ON THE FRONTIER

AMS PRESS
NEW YORK

On the Frontier

A MELODRAMA IN THREE ACTS

BY W. H. AUDEN *and*

CHRISTOPHER ISHERWOOD

RANDOM HOUSE · NEW YORK

Library of Congress Cataloging in Publication Data

Auden, Wystan Hugh, 1907-1973.
   On the frontier.

   Reprint of the 1938 ed. published by Random House,
New York.
   I. Isherwood, Christopher, 1904-   joint author.
II. Title.
PR6001.U405   1976   822'.9'12   75-41011
ISBN 0-404-14638-4

From the edition of 1938, New York
First AMS edition published in 1976
Manufactured in the United States of America

AMS PRESS INC.
NEW YORK, N.Y.

822,91
A8990

To

BENJAMIN BRITTEN

The drums tap out sensational bulletins;
Frantic the efforts of the violins
To drown the song behind the guarded hill:
The dancers do not listen; but they will.

CHARACTERS

Dr. Oliver Thorvald, *lecturer at a Westland university*

Hilda Thorvald, *his wife*

Eric Thorvald, *their son*

Martha Thorvald, *Dr. Thorvald's sister*

Colonel Hussek, *late of the Ostnian Army*

Louisa Vrodny, *his daughter*

Anna Vrodny, *her daughter*

Oswald Vrodny, *brother-in-law to Mrs. Vrodny*

Valerian, *head of the Westland Steel Trust*

Lessep, *his secretary*

Manners, *his butler*

Stahl, *a director of the Westland Steel Trust*

The Leader, *of Westland*

Storm-Trooper Grimm, *of the Leader's Bodyguard*

A Chorus of Eight, *five men and three women*

NOTES ON THE CHARACTERS

(All the Chorus must be able to sing)

DR. THORVALD: Middle-aged, pedantic, would have been a liberal under a democratic régime.

HILDA THORVALD: Good-natured, a bit slatternly. Has been the butterfly type. Hates rows. Wears dressing-jackets, kimonos, arty clothes.

ERIC THORVALD: Untidy, angular. About twenty.

MARTHA THORVALD: Violently repressed, fanatical. Wears glasses. Not to be played too broadly: remember that, beneath her fanaticism, she is an educated, intelligent woman. She is conscious of having a better brain than her sister-in-law.

COL. HUSSEK: An old lobster.

MRS. VRODNY: Embittered by poverty and household responsibilities; but with considerable reserves of power. The Vrodny-Hussek family has aristocratic traditions.

ANNA VRODNY: Must not be played as a mouse. She has character, but has hardly realised it.

OSWALD VRODNY: A cheerful ne'er-do-well. Might even speak with an Irish accent.

VALERIAN: Tall, suave, courteous, sardonic. Speaks precisely, with a slight foreign accent. About forty-five.

LESSEP: About twenty-seven. Intriguing. Can be spiteful. In dress and manner slightly pansy.

MANNERS: A stage butler.

STAHL: Though, with Valerian, he plays second fiddle, he is a man of considerable presence and power. He is not quite as tall as Valerian, but broader. About fifty-five.

THE LEADER: Try to avoid resemblances to living personages. The Leader wears a beard. He is about forty-five, anxious and ill. In the first act, he plays very stiffly, like a newsreel photograph of himself. His platform voice is like a trance-voice, loud and unnatural. He wears uniform throughout.

GRIMM: About twenty-five. Pale and tense. Wears uniform throughout.

SCENES

ACT ONE: EARLY SUMMER

Prologue: At the gates of the Valerian Works
Scene One: Valerian's Study
Interlude: A prison in Westland
Scene Two: The Ostnia-Westland Room

ACT TWO: A WEEK LATER

Scene One: The Ostnia-Westland Room
Interlude: A dance-hall in Westland
Scene Two: Valerian's Study

ACT THREE: NINE MONTHS LATER

Scene One: The Ostnia-Westland Room
Interlude: In the Westland Front Line
Scene Two: Valerian's Study (a fortnight later)
Interlude: The English Newspaper
Scene Three: The Ostnia-Westland Room

TIME: THE PRESENT

ACT ONE

(BEFORE THE CURTAIN)

[*Slow music. Eight workers—three women and five men —are grouped as if waiting for the gates of a factory to open. They sing in turn the following couplets:*]

The clock on the wall gives an electric tick,
I'm feeling sick, brother; I'm feeling sick.

The Sirens blow at eight; the sirens blow at noon;
Good-bye, sister, good-bye; we shall die soon.

Mr. Valerian has a mansion on the hill;
It's a long way to the grave, brother; a long way still.

The assembly-belt is like an army on the move;
It's stronger than hate, brother; it's stronger than
love.

The major came down with a pipe in his face;
Work faster, sister, faster, or you'll lose your place.

The major wears pointed shoes, and calls himself a
gent;
I'm behind with the rent, brother; I'm behind with
the rent.

The missus came in with her hair down, a-crying:
"Stay at home, George, stay at home, for baby's dying!"

There's grit in my lungs, there's sweat on my brow;
You were pretty once, Lisa, but oh, just look at you
    now!

You looked so handsome in your overalls of blue;
It was summer, Johnny, and I never knew.

My mother told me, when I was still a lad:
"Johnny, leave the girls alone." I wish I had.

The lathe on number five has got no safety-guard.
It's hard to lose your fingers, sister, mighty hard.

Went last night to the pictures; the girl was almost
    bare,
The boy spent a million dollars on that love-affair.

[*The factory siren sounds. The workers begin to move
across the stage and exit. The last verses are punctuated
by the sound of clocking-in.*]

When the hammer falls, the sparks fly up like stars;
If I were rich, brother, I'd have ten motor-cars.

Pass the word, sister, pass it along the line:
There's a meeting tonight at number forty-nine.

Oil that bearing, watch that dynamo;
When it's time to strike, brother, I'll let you know.

Stoke up the fires in furnace number three;
The day is coming, brother, when we shall all be free!

ACT ONE

SCENE I

[VALERIAN's study. VALERIAN's house is supposed to stand on high ground, overlooking the capital city of Westland. At the back of the stage there is a deep bay-window. The furniture is chiefly modern, but there are a number of statuettes and valuable etchings. A desk with telephones. A radiogram. Doors left and right.]

[When the curtain rises, MANNERS is arranging the chair-cushions, while LESSEP puts papers in order on the desk. It is a fine morning in early summer.]

LESSEP: Oh, by the way, Manners . . . your Master will be lunching on the terrace, this morning.

MANNERS Indeed, sir? Are those Mr. Valerian's orders, sir?

LESSEP [sharply]. Of course they're Mr. Valerian's orders. What did you suppose?

MANNERS. I beg your pardon, sir. I mention it only because Mr. Valerian has been accustomed to leave the management of this household entirely in my hands. This is the first time, in twelve years, that he has thought it necessary to say where he wished to lunch.

LESSEP. Well, it won't be the last time, I can assure you!

MANNERS. No, sir?

LESSEP. No!

[*Enter* VALERIAN.]

VALERIAN. Good morning, Lessep.

LESSEP. Good morning, Mr. Valerian.

VALERIAN. Are those ready for me to sign? [*Sees* MAN-NERS *is waiting.*] Yes, what is it?

MANNERS. Excuse me, sir. Am I to take it that you ordered lunch to be served on the terrace?

VALERIAN. Since when, Manners, have I given you orders about my meals? I am the master of this house, not the mistress.

MANNERS. Exactly, sir. Today I had thought of serving lunch in the Winter Garden. The terrace, in my humble opinion, would be too hot in this weather. The Leader, I am given to understand, dislikes the heat. But Mr. Lessep said—

VALERIAN. Mr. Lessep was mistaken. We bow to your judgment, Manners. The Winter Garden.

MANNERS. Thank you, sir.

[*Bows and exits.*]

LESSEP. Mr. Valerian . . . I hope you'll forgive me. . . .

VALERIAN. I can forgive anything, Lessep—except incompetence. Just now you behaved officiously, and tactlessly. Never mind. I am quite fairly satisfied with you, at present. As long as you continue to

be competent, I shall not have to bother the Ostnians for another secretary. . . .

LESSEP [*staggered*]. I . . . I don't think I quite understand. . . .

VALERIAN. No? Then I will speak more plainly. You
are in the employ of the Ostnian Steel Com-
bine. . . . Oh, pray don't suppose that you are the
first! Despite the general identity of our interests,
it is a regrettable fact that the Ostnian industrialists do not trust us—and that we, I am sorry to say,
do not entirely trust the Ostnians. So we both prefer to rely on inside information. . . . It is an ar-
rangement which suits me very well. All I ask is
that the employees the Ostnians send us (always
by the most devious routes) shall be efficient. We
also have sent them some admirable secretaries. . . .
Now, do we understand each other?

LESSEP. Mr. Valerian, on my word of honour—

VALERIAN [*signing papers*]. Very well. I have no time
for arguments. I am not asking for a confession. . . .
Oh, one more little point: yesterday, you took
from my safe the plans of the new Valerian tank
and photographed them. Clumsily. You are not accustomed to this kind of work, I think? It requires
practice.

LESSEP. I'm ready to swear that I never touched—

VALERIAN [*still writing*]. Yes, yes. Of course. . . . But in
order that you shall not commit a gaffe which
might seriously prejudice your prospects with your
employers, let me tell you that we have already sold

this tank to the Ostnian War Office.... You didn't know? Too stupid, isn't it? Lack of departmental co-operation, as always. It will be the ruin of both our countries....

LESSEP [*collapsing*]. I'd better leave at once....

VALERIAN. Nonsense! You will learn. . . . No tears, I beg! They bore me indescribably. . . . We have wasted four minutes on an exceedingly dull subject. . . . And now tell me, please: what are my appointments for today?

LESSEP [*pulling himself together with an effort*]. Mr. Stahl is coming in to see you at twelve-thirty. He will remain to meet the Leader, at lunch. This afternoon you will accompany the Leader on his inspection of the Works. And you wanted, if possible, to get away in time for the Poussin auction, at four forty-five....

VALERIAN. Ah, to be sure—the Poussins! The one bright moment of a dreary day! I mustn't miss them on any account. And the Leader will speak for an hour, at least. . . . Please arrange an interruption. At the first opportunity, our operatives are to burst spontaneously into the National Hymn. Spontaneously, mind you. . . . It's the only known method of cutting short the Leader's flow of imperatives.

LESSEP. I'll see to it, Mr. Valerian.

VALERIAN. You'd better go down there now, and talk to some of our foremen. They're accustomed to organize these things.

LESSEP. Is there anything else?

VALERIAN. Nothing, thank you.

LESSEP [*prepares to go, hesitates*]. Mr. Valerian—I just want to say: I shall never forget your generosity. . . .

VALERIAN. My dear boy, I am never generous—as you will very soon discover, to your cost. Please do not flatter yourself that your conscience and its scruples interest me in the very slightest degree. In this establishment, there is no joy over the sinner that repents. . . . Very well. You may go.

> [*Exit* LESSEP. VALERIAN *goes thoughtfully up stage to the window, and stands looking out over the city.*]

VALERIAN. The Valerian Works. . . . How beautiful they look from here! Much nicer than the cathedral next door. . . . A few people still go there to pray, I suppose—peasants who have only been in the city a generation, middle-class women who can't get husbands. . . . Curious to think that it was once the centre of popular life. If I had been born in the thirteenth century, I suppose I should have wanted to be a bishop. [*Factory sirens, off, sound the lunch-hour.*] Now my sirens have supplanted his bells. But the crowd down there haven't changed much. The dole is as terrifying as hell-fire—probably worse. . . . Run along, little man. Lunch is ready for you in the Valerian Cafeteria. Why so anxious? You shall have every care. You may spoon in the Valerian Park, and buy the ring next day at the Valerian Store. Then you shall settle down in a cosy Valerian villa, which, I assure you, has been highly praised by architectural experts. The Valerian School, equipped with the very latest apparatus, will educate your dear little kiddies in Patriotism and Personal Hygiene. A smart Valerian Family Runabout will take you on Sundays to pinic by the waterfall, along with several hundred others of your kind. The Valerian Bank will look after your savings, if any; our doctors will see to your health, and our funeral parlours will bury you. . . And then you talk about Socialism! Oh, yes, I am well aware that university professors, who ought to know better, have assured you that you are the heir to all the ages. Nature's last and most daring experiment. Believe them, by all means, if it helps you to forget the whip. Indulge in all the longings that aspirin and sweet tea and stump oratory can arouse. Dream of your never-never land, where the parks are covered with naked cow-like women, quite free; where the rich are cooked over a slow fire, and pigeons coo from the cupolas. Let the band in my park convince you that Life is seriously interested in marital fidelity and the right use of leisure, in the reign of happiness and peace. Go on, go on. Think what you like, vote for whom you like. What difference does it make? Make your little protest. Get a new master if you can. You will soon be made to realize that he is as exacting as the old, and probably less intelligent. . . . The truth is, Nature is not interested in underlings—in the lazy, the inefficient, the self-indulgent, the People. Nor, for that matter, in the Aristocracy, which is now only another name for the Idle Rich. The idle are never powerful. With their gigolos and quack doctors, they are as unhappy as the working classes who can afford neither, and a great deal more bored. The world has never been governed by the People or by the merely Rich, and it never will be. It is governed by men like myself—though, in practice, we are usually rich and often come from the People.

[*He moves away from the window to the desk and picks up a signed photograph of the Leader.*]

No, not by you, dear Leader. You're one of the People, really, which is why they love you, you poor muddle-headed bundle of nerves, so overworked and so hypnotized by the sound of your own voice that you will never know what's happening nor who pulls the strings. Do you think, my modern Caesar, that the Roman emperors were important? They weren't. It was the Greek freedmen, who kept the accounts, who mattered. The cardinals mattered in the Middle Ages, not those dreary feudal barons.

[*He picks up a statuette.*]

No, perhaps that's wrong, too. Real political power is only made possible by electricity, double entry and high explosives. Perhaps, after all, the hermits and the artists were wiser. Nothing is worth while except complete mastery, and, in those days, that could only be achieved over the Self. I wonder what it felt like to be St. Francis Stylites or Poussin. Well, times have changed. The arts haven't been important since the eighteenth century. Today, a creative man becomes an engineer or a scientist, not an artist. He leaves that career to neurotics and humbugs who can't succeed at anything else. [*Back at the window.*] This is probably the last period of human history. The political régimes of the future may have many fancy names, but never again will the common man be allowed to rule his own life or judge for himself. To be an artist or a saint has ceased to be modern. . . . Yes, for the man of power, there can now be but one aim—absolute control of mankind.

[*Enter* MANNERS.]

MANNERS. Mr. Stahl, sir.

[*Enter* STAHL.]

VALERIAN. Ah, my dear Stahl, welcome home! [*Exit* MANNERS.]

STAHL. How are you, Valerian? You're looking well. [*Looks round the room.*] It seems strange to be in this room again. . . . You've bought a new etching, I see.

VALERIAN. Oh, I have a great deal to show you. But that can wait. You had a pleasant journey, I hope?

STAHL. Thanks, yes. Excellent.

VALERIAN. You only got back yesterday morning?

STAHL. And I've been run off my feet ever since!

VALERIAN. Your wife is well, I trust?

24

STAHL. Not as well as I should like. She's been suffering a lot with her migraine, lately. Extraordinary thing, migraine. Nobody really understands it. She stayed on in Paris to see that new Swedish man; he's discovered a special injection. I hope it'll do her some good.

VALERIAN. I am truly sorry to hear this. . . . And your boy? I hope his studies are progressing favourably?

STAHL. Well . . . yes and no. Igor works hard enough, but he's so undecided. He wants to give up engineering and read Icelandic. . . . I suppose it's just a phase. . . .

VALERIAN. My dear Stahl, you are indeed the model family man! Your worries never cease!

STAHL. Upon my word, Valerian, I sometimes envy you. When one sees you in this charming house, surrounded by your treasures, with no wife to run up milliners' bills! The world looks black enough, these days, heaven knows—but at least a bachelor has only himself to think of. . . .

VALERIAN. Always the pessimist! Which reminds me that I haven't yet thanked you for all those admirably lucid and exceedingly depressing letters. . . .

STAHL. Well, I'm glad, at any rate, that you found them lucid!

VALERIAN. So much so that, as soon as I heard you were returning, I arranged for the Leader to come and hear the worst from Cassandra's own lips. There is nothing he so much enjoys as bad news—about foreign countries: England doomed, Germany bankrupt, the United States heading for her last and greatest slump. . . . Mind you lay it on thick! And with particular emphasis on the contrast between decadent, anarchical Ostnia and our own dear Westland—that paradise of solvency and order.

STAHL. I only hope the food won't choke me as I say it!

VALERIAN. My dear friend, you can have confidence in my chef: Ananias himself could lunch here with perfect impunity. . . . Though really it's a wonder I wasn't suffocated myself, the other evening: I had to spend an hour praising the works of the new National Academy of Art—Putensen, de Kloot, and those exquisite little landscapes (or should I say "cowscapes"?) of Ketchling. . . .

STAHL. Ketchling? But surely he's the man who does the hair-tonic advertisements?

VALERIAN. What a memory you have! A rather dangerous memory, if I may say so, for these times. . . . Yes, it all happened about three months ago. You were in Brazil, I believe. Poor Milnik was so unfortunate as to offend the Minister of Propaganda. Next morning, he was discovered to possess an Ostnian great-grandmother, and, within a week, Ketchling had stepped into his shoes. . . . Ketchling's wife, I may add, had been having an affair with our respected Postmaster-General. . . .

STAHL. The Postmaster? But surely Madame Korteniz . . . ?

VALERIAN. The reign of Madame Korteniz has ended,

26

quite suddenly, under rather amusing circumstances. . . . But that's a long story, which will keep. Here I am, gossiping away like an old concierge, and you have told me nothing about your journey! First of all, how does Westland appear to a returned traveller—sadly provincial, I fear? There have been changes since you left, and none of them for the better. Since the Leader's newest statue was unveiled, it has become necessary to walk down Victory Avenue with one's eyes tightly closed. I always tell my chauffeur to make a detour. . . .

STAHL. Yes, I've seen that monstrosity already. . . . But I'm sorry to say that, since my return, I've received even worse shocks—

VALERIAN. Ah, you mean the neo-Egyptian portico of the new Culture House? Well, it's a nice point. The Leader, you'll admit, is the uglier of the two; but the Culture House is so much larger. . . .

STAHL. There's more wrong with this country than its architecture, Valerian. You know that better than I do. Coming back like this, after six months, one's appalled, simply appalled by the way things are going. Of course, I haven't had time to make detailed enquiries, yet; but I talked to the works managers early this morning, and yesterday I was at the Stock Exchange and around the clubs. People are afraid to say much, naturally; but I drew my own conclusions.

VALERIAN. Which were, no doubt, as gloomy as usual?

I shall listen to them with the greatest interest. But not, my dear Stahl, *not* before lunch! You will ruin both our appetites.

STAHL. I know that it amuses you to be flippant. But these are facts. You can't pass them by, like the Leader's statue, with your eyes shut. . . . Something must be done, and done quickly. We're in for really big trouble. Conditions at the labour camps are getting worse all the time. The men are complaining quite openly; six months ago, they wouldn't have dared. The food isn't fit for an African village. The buildings leak—what can you expect from that Army contract stuff? T.B. is definitely on the increase. As for the Shock Troops—if even fifty per cent of what I hear is true—the whole organization's rotten from top to bottom; and the commandants are responsible only to the Leader—which means to nobody at all. If you want to see them on business, you must search the night-clubs and the brothels; they never go near their offices. At the barracks, you'll hear the same story: the Leader has broken every promise he ever made. The same thing down at the Works. Agitators have been getting at the men, secret unions are being formed. I even heard rumours of a stay-in strike. . . .

VALERIAN. My dear friend, your sojourn in the democratic countries seems to have confused your ideas a little! Surely you are aware that here, in our happy Westland, the Leader has declared all strikes illegal?

STAHL. An illegal strike is simply an insurrection.

VALERIAN. Which can be dealt with as such.

STAHL. Which *cannot* be dealt with! You know as well
as I do that the troops would refuse to fire. Why,
the General Staff wouldn't even dare to give the
order!

VALERIAN. Aren't we becoming rather melodramatic?
Do you, seriously, in your heart of hearts, believe
that things could ever come to shooting? In Russia, yes. In Spain, yes. Never in Westland. You
know our countrymen; a nation of grumblers—and
grumblers are never dangerous. The situation is
bad, of course—disgraceful, appalling, but hardly
serious. When you have been at home a week or
two, you will recapture that peculiar Westland
sense of proportion—as lop-sided as Putensen's
nudes—and you will agree with me.

STAHL. Perhaps I shall. Yes . . . that's just what I'm
afraid of. . . . But now, before I begin to squint like
the rest of you, let me tell you that, in my con-
sidered opinion, this country is on the verge of a
revolution!

VALERIAN. Revolution! Revolution! Eternally that
bogey word! When the old Emperor abdicated,
everybody predicted a revolution, and what did we
get? A cabinet of shopkeepers in ill-fitting top
hats, who misquoted Marx and scrambled to culti-
vate the society of effete aristocrats, whose titles
they themselves had just abolished by decree. The
workers were impressed by their socialist speeches,

and tried to act upon them—so the shopkeeper-marxists called them bolsheviks and traitors, dissolved parliament, suppressed the unions, and established a dictatorship which lacked nothing but a dictator. Then came the Leader, in his fancy-dress uniform, and these same shopkeepers rejoiced, because the National Revolution was to make an end of the Valerian Works and all the big business concerns and open the garden of paradise to the small trader. And what did the Leader do? Crying: "Revolution!" he obligingly ruined a number of our lesser competitors and business rivals. He did not dare to touch the Valerian Trust. He did not want to touch it. Without us, he could not exist for a fortnight. . . . As for the workers, who you so much dread—they play at secret meetings, of which I am informed, and at printing illegal pamphlets, which litter my desk at this moment. The workers are all patient sheep, or silly crowing cockerels, or cowardly rabbits. . . .

[*Enter* MANNERS.]

MANNERS. I beg your pardon, sir. The Leader's Bodyguard has arrived. They wish to make the—ah, usual inspection.

STAHL. Good Heavens! Whatever for?

VALERIAN. Oh, you will soon get used to these little formalities. A month ago, there was another attempt on the Leader's life. Hushed up, naturally. But I thought the foreign press would have got hold of it. Since then, precautions have been doubled. The Leader never visits a strange house without assuring himself that there are no assassins hiding on the premises. . . . Very well. Let one of them come in.

> [MANNERS *exits for a moment and re-enters with Storm-Trooper* GRIMM.]

GRIMM [*giving Westland Salute*]. For Westland. . . . I have orders to search this floor.

VALERIAN. By all means. Please make yourself quite at home.

GRIMM [*indicating door, left*]. Where does that door lead to?

VALERIAN. To my bedroom, my bathroom, and the back staircase. . . . But, surely, you've been here before?

GRIMM. I only joined the Bodyguard last week.

VALERIAN. I see. . . . Strange. I seem to remember your face.

GRIMM [*quickly*]. That's impossible. I come from the eastern province.

VALERIAN. Well, we all make mistakes. . . . Pray don't let me detain you from your duties. And don't forget to look under the bed.

> [GRIMM *salutes and exits.*]

VALERIAN [*to* MANNERS]. You'd better go with him, I think. He might take a fancy to my silver hair-brushes.

> [MANNERS *bows and exits.*]

VALERIAN. There goes one of the rulers of our country!

STAHL. Common gangsters!

VALERIAN. After all, there is a good deal to be said for
· gangsters. One's dealings with them are so charm-
ingly simple. They understand two things: money
and the whip. They know where their bread and
butter comes from. The Leader is much safer with
these boys than with a pack of crooked politicians.

STAHL. By the way, how is the Leader, nowadays? In
Paris, there was a lot of talk about his—health.

VALERIAN. With good reason, I'm afraid. You know,
three weeks ago, he had a very serious breakdown.
I'm told Pegoud was sent for. . . .

STAHL. Whew! So he's really mad, at last!

VALERIAN. My dear friend, the Leader has always been
mad. The really alarming symptom is that he's
beginning to recover. The crises are becoming iso-
lated, less predictable, much more violent. He is
no longer the roaring waterfall, whose power could
be utilized and whose noise was harmless. He is
the volcano which may suddenly destroy cities and
men. . . . I ought to warn you: if any little disturb-
ance occurs during lunch, please appear to take no
notice. And, when it is over, behave as if nothing
had happened. . . .

STAHL. A nice party you've let me in for, I must say!
I'm beginning to feel quite scared. . . . I've only
spoken to the Leader twice in my life. I'd no idea
you knew him so intimately.

VALERIAN. I've been seeing a good deal of him, lately.
He interests me. I have been studying, as the
Americans say, the secret of his success.

STAHL. And what is this secret?

VALERIAN. The Leader, you see, is our national martyr. We Westlanders are a stolid, insensitive race; we need someone to do our suffering for us. The Leader bears upon his shoulders all the wrongs, all the griefs that Westland ever suffered—and many more besides. When the fat placid housewives attend his meetings, and see him rave and wring his hands, and tremble and weep, they shake their heads in their motherly way, and murmur: "Poor Leader—he is going through all this for *us!*" Then they return to their tea, with whipped cream and apple cakes, purged and ennobled, by proxy.

STAHL. But what beats me is how one can have any kind of personal relationship with him. Why, he isn't a man at all! He's a gramophone!

VALERIAN. No doubt. But even a gramophone can be made to play better and more harmonious records. . . . As a matter of fact, your mentioning gramophones was unintentionally apt. The Leader often drops in to listen to mine.

STAHL. You mean to say that you actually *play* to him!

VALERIAN. Oh, yes, indeed. Like Orpheus. Whenever he seems tired and dispirited, or the conversation flags. . . . I flatter myself that I am educating him, slowly but surely. . . . We started with *Narcissus* and the *Melody in F*. After a fortnight, he was getting tired of them, so I prescribed *The War March of the Priests*—all too successfully. I think even

33

Mendelssohn himself would have wished he had never written it. . . . At length, we passed on to the *Pathetic Symphony*, and, I am happy to say, out-grew it at the end of a weary month. At present, Rameau's *Tambourin* is the favourite. It seems likely to last through the summer. . . .

STAHL. Really, Valerian, you've missed your vocation! You should have been a lion-tamer!

[*Enter* MANNERS.]

MANNERS. The Leader has arrived, sir.

STAHL. Good gracious! He nearly caught us talking high treason!

[*Noises off. Someone shouts: "Guard! Attention!" The Leader's voice is heard, saying: "For Westland!" Enter* THE LEADER. MANNERS *exits, behind him.*]

LEADER [*salutes*]. For Westland! [*Shakes hands*] How are you, Valerian?

VALERIAN. Delighted to see you, sir. . . . I believe you know Mr. Stahl, one of our directors?

STAHL. You will hardly remember me, my Leader. We met last at the Industrial Banquet.

LEADER. I never forget a face. [*Salutes.*] For Westland!

VALERIAN. I hope we see you in good health?

[*Enter* MANNERS, *with cocktails.*]

LEADER. My health is at the service of my country. Therefore it is good.

[MANNERS *hands round cocktails, and exits.*]

VALERIAN. May it long continue so! Mr. Stahl, as I told you in my letter, has just returned from a business

34

tour of Europe and America. I wanted you to hear
his impressions.

STAHL. There are certain points which might possibly
interest you, my Leader.

LEADER. Everything interests me. When I study any
subject, I acquaint myself with its smallest details.
[*Raising his glass*] Westland!

VALERIAN ⎱ [*both drinking*]. Westland!
STAHL ⎰

LEADER [*to* STAHL]. Tell me, is it true that, in London,
Negroes are even permitted to play in the dance
orchestras?

STAHL. Well—yes, certainly.

LEADER. I was right! Only a dying race could show such
tolerance. England is becoming a foreign colony.
Very soon, they'll be having Ostnians in to drive
the trams! Ha, ha, ha!

[VALERIAN *and* STAHL *laugh dutifully.*]
[*Enter* MANNERS.]

MANNERS. Lunch is served, sir.

[*Exit.*]

LEADER. I am in good spirits today! What beautiful
weather! We shall have a real Westland summer!
Valerian, I have a surprise for you. After inspect-
ing your Works, I shall take you for a drive in the
park.

VALERIAN [*suppressing a groan*]. That will be delight-
ful! Shall we go downstairs?

LEADER [*ignoring him*]. I want to have young faces
around me—youth, health, springtime. The per-

35

fume of the flowers. The smell of the trees. The lithe active bodies of our splendid Westland children. . . . Ah, it does one good!

VALERIAN. I can imagine no more charming way of spending the afternoon. . . . Perhaps you'd like to have lunch? Then we can start earlier on our programme. . . .

LEADER [*as before*]. I was thinking, too, that we might visit your model cottages. I am never so happy as when I can spare a few moments from my work to spend among the common people. How delighted and surprised they will be to have their Leader among them! I love to watch their contented smiles as they bend over their humble tasks, working proudly, for Westland, each in his own sphere. How well I understand them! How well I know their wants! I know what they are thinking even before they know it themselves. It is my mission to restore to every Westlander the dignity of labour, to put good honest tools into his hands, to guard him from crafty, underhand foreign competition. Westland must awake! Westland must throw off her fetters! Westland must raise the heavy load of poverty from the shoulders of the groaning poor. [*He picks up a paper-weight from the desk.*] Westland must—

VALERIAN [*tactfully taking the paper-weight from the Leader's hand*]. Bravo, sir! Bravo! I hope you'll say that to our operatives this afternoon. It will inspire them. . . . Lunch is ready. Shall we go down?

36

LEADER [*suddenly cut short in the middle of his enthu-siasm, stares stupidly, for a moment, at his empty hand. Then, as if coming to earth, he says quietly*]. Ah, yes—lunch. . . .

CURTAIN

(BEFORE THE CURTAIN)

[A ray of light, barred with shadow, as if through a prison window, illuminates four prisoners, two women and two men. They are squatting on the ground, hand-cuffed. Their faces are ghastly.]

[Air: "Sweet Betsy from Pike."]

FIRST PRISONER [sings].

Industrialists, bankers, in comfortable chairs
Are saying: "We still have control of affairs.
The Leader will have all our enemies shot."

ALL. They would like to forget us, but, oh, they cannot!

SECOND PRISONER.

The idle, the rich, and the shabby genteel,
And the clever who think that the world isn't
real
Say: "The forces of order have triumphed!
We're safe!"

ALL. But the world has its views on how to behave!

THIRD PRISONER.

The judge sits on high in a very fine wig,
He talks about Law and he talks very big,
And chaplains in church say: "Obedience is best."

ALL. We've heard that before and we're not much impressed!

FOURTH PRISONER.
The Leader stands up on his platform and shouts:
"Follow me and you never need have any doubts!
Put on my uniform, wave my great flag!"

ALL. But when the wind blows he shall burst like a bag!

FIRST PRISONER.
"If you're foolish enough," they declare, "to resist,
You shall feel the full weight of fieldboot and fist."
They beat us with truncheons; they cast us in jail,

ALL. But all their forms of persuasion shall fail!

SECOND PRISONER.
They boast: "We shall last for a thousand long
years,"
But History, it happens, has other ideas.
"We shall live on for ever!" they cry, but instead

ALL. They shall die soon defending the cause of the
dead!

THIRD PRISONER.
They talk of the mystical value of Blood,
Of War as a holy and purifying flood,
Of bullets and bombs as the true works of art.

ALL. They'll change their opinion when shot through
the heart!

FOURTH PRISONER.
Perhaps we shall die by a firing-squad,

Perhaps they will kill us, that wouldn't be odd,
But when we lie down with the earth on our face
ALL. There'll be ten more much better to fight in our
place!
The night may seem lonely, the night may seem
long,
But Time is patient and that's where they're
wrong!
For Truth shall flower and Error explode
And the people be free then to choose their own
road!

BLACK OUT

ACT ONE

SCENE II

[The Ostnia-Westland Room. It is not to be supposed
that the Frontier between the two countries does actually pass through this room: the scene is only intended to
convey the idea of the Frontier—the left half of the stage
being in Westland: the right half being in Ostnia. The
furnishing of the two halves should suggest differences
in national characteristics, and also in the nature of the
two families which inhabit them: the Thorvalds' (Westland) home is academic; the Vrodney-Hussek (Ostnian)
home is comfortable, reactionary, bourgeois. Each home
has a door and window, left and right respectively. On
the back wall of each hangs a big portrait, with a wireless set standing beneath it. The Thorvalds have a portrait of the Westland "Leader," who is bearded and
ferocious-looking: the Vrodny-Hussek family have a
portrait of the King of Ostnia, very suave and gracious,
with orders and much gold braid. The chairs are arranged in two semi-circles, and the concentration of
lighting should heighten the impression of an invisible
barrier between the two halves of the stage. The two
groups of characters (with the exceptions to be noted later) seem absolutely unaware of each other's existence.]
[It is evening. When the curtain rises, DR.

OLIVER THORVALD, *the university professor, is writing at his desk.* MRS. THORVALD *is laying cards at a table, and* ERIC *their son, who is a student, sits writing in an armchair with a book-rest. On the other side of the stage,* MRS. VRODNY *is darning socks, seated on the sofa. Her father,* COLONEL HUSSEK, *sits reading the newspaper in an invalid wheel-chair.*]

DR. THORVALD [*pausing to read aloud what he has written*]. "Professor Jongden appears to have modelled his style upon the more sensational articles in the popular press of his country. For his scholarship, however, we can discover no precedent. His emendations would not convince a commercial traveller. The authorities he quotes, and as frequently misquotes, are most of them out of date. Beyer's great work on the Ionian Laws he does not so much as mention; no doubt he is unwilling to acknowledge that any contribution to culture could be made by a nation which he has always been taught to regard as barbarian."

COL. HUSSEK [*reading from newspaper*]. "The Minister for Propaganda has banned the sale in Ostnia of the Westland *Sunday Sun* for one month—as the result of the insulting caricatures of His Majesty, published in last Sunday's issue. . . ." I can't think what the country's coming to! Thirty years ago, they wouldn't have dared! The old King must turn in his grave. He would never have allowed our honour to be—

MRS. VRODNY [*bitterly*]. Nobody cares about honour, these days! All they think of now is Self!

COL. HUSSEK. You're right, Louisa! Our young people have no sense of Ostnian loyalty.

MRS. VRODNY. You've no idea, Father, how rude the shopgirls are, nowadays! I could smack their faces sometimes; they're so insolent. And the prices! Mother would have had a fit! [*Holds up a sock with an enormous hole in it.*] Just look at that! How Oswald manages to wear his socks into such holes I can't imagine!

DR. THORVALD [*reading aloud*]. "We strongly advise the Professor to leave the classics alone and to betake himself to a sphere to which his talents are less unfitted. We suggest that the scandals of the Ostnian Court would be a suitable choice."

ERIC. Who are you attacking this time, Father?

DR. THORVALD. Jongden has just brought out a book on Ionia—a typical Ostnian piece of work. All superficial brilliance and fluff, with nothing behind it. No Ostnian ever made a scholar. They think it vulgar to take trouble.

ERIC. But isn't he the man who's been offered a chair at Yale?

DR. THORVALD. Just because he can make amusing little speeches after dinner, they prefer him to a real scholar, like Beyer! It's preposterous! He can't hold a candle to him!

MRS. THORVALD. You know, dear, it's only because Beyer is a Westlander. And they believe all the lies their newspapers spread about us. I can't understand why they're allowed to print such stuff. The Leader ought to put a stop to it.

COL. HUSSEK. Tcha! Another lightning strike at the Docks! If they'd only shoot a few of them, it'd put a stop to all this nonsense!

MRS. VRODNY. I'm sure it's only due to Westland agitators, Father. The Ostnian working man would never behave like that of his own accord. He's got too much common sense. He knows it only puts up the cost of living.

MRS. THORVALD. The Ace of Diamonds. . . . Do you think that means I've won a prize in the *Sunday Sun* Doublets, or only that Martha's ordered enough vegetables to go round? She so seldom does. . . . Eric dear, I do wish you wouldn't work so hard! I'm sure it can't be good for you. Why don't you go out and do field-exercises, like the other students?

DR. THORVALD. Leave the boy alone, Hilda. You can't become a scholar without keeping your nose to the grindstone, eh, Eric? [*Rises from desk and comes over to* ERIC's *chair, lighting his pipe.*] What are you writing on, this time? [*Looks over* ERIC's *shoulder.*] "The chances of European peace!" What a ridiculous subject! Surely Professor Bluteisen never set you that?

ERIC. No. I'm doing it for a few of my friends. Some of us are trying to think these things out.

DR. THORVALD. You're wasting your time, my boy.

What chances are there of peace—with the Ostnians arming to the teeth? I tell you, Europe's a powder-magazine. It only needs a spark.

Mrs. Thorvald. Martha says the war's coming this year. It's all in Revelations, she says. She tried to explain it to me, but she's so difficult to understand: her false teeth fit so badly.

Eric. Don't talk like that, Mother! Of course there'll be a war if we all go on saying and thinking there will be, and doing nothing to stop it. Why are we all so frightened? None of us *want* war.

Mrs. Thorvald. We don't, but what about the Ostnians?

Col. Hussek. Notes. Negotiations. . . . We're too polite to them; that's our trouble!

Mrs. Vrodny. The Westlander's a bully. Always has been.

Dr. Thorvald. After the last war, when we were weak, they bullied us. And it's only now, when the Leader's shown them that Westland won't stand any nonsense, that they've learnt to mind their p's and q's a bit.

Col. Hussek. The only thing the Westlander understands is the stick. We ought to have finished the job properly, last time.

Eric. How do you know the Ostnians want war?

Mrs. Thorvald. Haven't they always hated us? Haven't they always been jealous of us? Especially since our national revolution.

DR. THORVALD. They're jealous of our liberty and power of creative progress.

MRS. VRODNY. The trouble is, they've no traditions. That's why they're jealous of us. They always have been. They're spoilt children, really.

DR. THORVALD. A decadent race is always jealous of a progressive one.

MRS. VRODNY. You may say what you like; tradition and breeding count.

MRS. THORVALD. You may say what you like, Eric. You can't wipe out the history of a thousand years.

COL. HUSSEK. Damned bolsheviks!

ERIC. Well, I think that if people—the ordinary decent people in both countries—would only get together, we could . . . .

> [Enter ANNA VRODNY, with a shopping basket. The effect of her presence upon ERIC is instantly noticeable. He breaks off in the middle of his sentence, as though he had forgotten what it was he had meant to say. Throughout the rest of the scene he follows ANNA's movements eagerly with his eyes. ANNA, also, is watching ERIC, but more timidly and covertly. Nobody else on the stage appears to notice this.]

MRS. VRODNY. Oh, there you are at last, Anna! Whatever have you been doing all this time?

DR. THORVALD. Could what, Eric?

ANNA. I'm sorry, Mother. There was such a queue at Benets'.

[*Begins to take parcels out of basket and lay them on the table.*]

DR. THORVALD. Well, go on! What could you do?

MRS. THORVALD. Oh, don't argue so, Oliver! It makes my head ache!

DR. THORVALD. Sorry, my dear. I was only trying to make him see how woolly-minded he is. And Westland has no use for woolliness, these days. I've got to go now to a meeting of the tutorial board, to consider the case of those so-called pacifist demonstrators yesterday. And I don't mind telling you, Eric, that I shall vote for their expulsion from the University. Let that be a warning to you, my boy!

[*Exit* DR. THORVALD.]

MRS. VRODNY [*rising from the sofa to inspect* ANNA's *purchases*]. You call that a chicken? Why didn't you go to Litvak's?

ANNA. But, Mother, you said Litvak's was so expensive!

MRS. VRODNY. Oh, it's hopeless! I can't trust any of you to do the simplest things! I work my fingers to the bone for you all, and nobody helps me in the least!

MRS. THORVALD. The Queen of Hearts! Well, I never! At my age! It must be for you, Eric! How exciting!

MRS. VRODNY. Don't stand there dawdling, Anna! We've got to get supper ready. It'll be late as it is.

[MRS. VRODNY *and* ANNA *collect the parcels and exeunt. During the scene which follows,* COL. HUSSEK *falls gradually asleep.*]

MRS. THORVALD. The cards never lie! Eric, I don't believe you're listening!

47

ERIC. Sorry, Mother, I was just thinking about something.

> [*Enter* MARTHA THORVALD, *Dr. Thorvald's sister, with a prayer-book and a bunch of flowers. She pauses solemnly, before speaking to salute the Leader's portrait.*]

MARTHA. Cards again? Really, Hilda, I'm surprised at you, indulging in that sinful nonsense!

MRS. THORVALD. Oh, Martha! It isn't nonsense!

MARTHA [*arranging flowers in a vase before the LEADER's portrait*]. It's wicked superstition. . . . There! Don't these look beautiful, under the Leader's picture? They're just the colour of his eyes! Pastor Brock preached a wonderful sermon about him today. . . .

MRS. THORVALD. The Pastor's such a fine man, but I do wish he wouldn't shout so. He makes my head ache.

MARTHA. Westland needs more like him! He took as his text: "I come not to bring peace, but a sword!"

ERIC. Pastor Brock isn't a Christian at all. He wants to rewrite the Bible.

MARTHA. Eric! How dare you!

ERIC. "They that live by the sword shall perish by the sword." How does he explain that?

MARTHA. I suppose you think you're clever: sitting there and sneering, while every decent young Westlander is out learning to defend his country? If I were your mother—

48

Mrs. Thorvald. Oh, my poor head! If you two are going to quarrel, I'm off to bed.

[*Exit* Mrs. Thorvald.]

Eric. I'm sorry, Aunt Martha. I didn't mean to hurt your feelings.

Martha. Don't apologize to me. Apologize to the Leader. It's him you hurt when you talk like that. He cares so much for all of us. . . . Good night, my Leader! God keep you!

[*She salutes the picture and exits.*]

Eric [*rises from his chair, goes up to the picture and regards it*]. Tell me, what is it you really want? Why do you make that fierce face? You're not fierce, really. You have eyes like my father's. Are you lonely, are you unhappy, behind that alarming beard? Yes, I see you are. Perhaps you only want love—like me. . . .

[*He continues to examine the picture.*]

Col. Hussek [*waking up with a violent start*]. Extend on the right! Rapid fire! Charge! [*Rubbing his eyes.*] Louisa! [*Enter* Mrs. Vrodny.] Where's my supper?

Mrs. Vrodny. We're waiting for Oswald.

Col. Hussek. Boozing again, I suppose!

Mrs. Vrodny. It's always the same thing, when he gets his pension money.

[*Oswald's voice is heard singing, outside.*]
Here he is, at last!

[*Enter* Oswald Vrodny, *drunk.*]

Oswald. [*singing*]. Then up spoke Captain O'Hara:

"It's a hundred and one in the shade;
If you give me your Irish whisky
You can keep your Irish maid!"

Well, Louisa, and how are the busy little fingers,
this evening? Good evening, General Fieldboots!
Still fighting to the last man?

COL. HUSSEK. You're drunk, sir!

OSWALD [*producing a bottle*]. I've brought you some
powerful reinforcements! Guess what this is!

MRS. VRODNY [*trying to snatch bottle*]. Give me that at
once!

OSWALD. Naughty! Mustn't snatch! Allow me to in-
troduce you to an old friend you haven't seen for
a very long time—the finest Westland whisky!

COL. HUSSEK. How dare you bring their filthy stuff into
this house!

MRS. VRODNY. It's so unpatriotic!

OSWALD. Patriotism be damned! I can't touch that foul
Ostnian cognac; sooner drink cold tea! What good
is it going to do Ostnia if I ruin my liver? Answer
me that! You and your patriotism! Those chaps
over there know how to make whisky, and I'm
grateful to them! Any man who makes good whisky
is my friend for life! [*Drinks.*] Here's to Westland!

COL. HUSSEK. Another word, sir, and I'll call the police
and have you arrested, this minute!

MRS. VRODNY. Father and I have been very patient
with you. But there's a limit to everything. You've
never done a hand's turn in your life! You're just a
drunken sponger!

[*Enter* ANNA. ERIC *immediately turns from the picture, and begins to watch her, as before, but with increasing agitation.*]

ANNA. Mother! Mother! Do be quiet, please. All the neighbours will hear you! Come on, Uncle Oswald. Supper's ready in the kitchen.

OSWALD. [*taking* ANNA's *arm*] That's my own little girl!

ANNA. You two go on. I'll look after him.

[*Exeunt* MRS. VRODNY, *wheeling* COL. HUSSEK. ANNA *follows, half-supporting* OSWALD, *who is humming the Wedding March from Lohengrin.*]

ERIC [*taking a pace forward, exclaims involuntarily, despairingly*] Anna!

[*But* ANNA *does not seem to hear him. Exeunt* ANNA *and* OSWALD. ERIC *stands looking sadly after her.*]

CURTAIN

ACT TWO

ACT TWO

SCENE I

[*The Ostnia-Westland Room. It is evening. As the curtain rises, we see on the left of the stage,* DR. THORVALD, MRS. THORVALD, MARTHA *and* ERIC, *drinking a bedtime cup of tea.* ERIC, *as usual, is watching* ANNA VRODNY, *who sits sewing on the right of the stage, with* OSWALD *and* COL. HUSSEK. COL. HUSSEK *has the newspaper.* OSWALD *is lazily smoking. Both wireless sets are switched on, but silent.*]

ANNA. Please come to bed, Grandpa. It's after eleven. You look tired out.

COL. HUSSEK. Nonsense, my dear! Never felt better in my life! Must wait to hear the news. Westland will have to admit responsibility. She can't get round the evidence. I tell you, this means war!

OSWALD. Thank God I'm fat and fifty! No more wars for us, Colonel! We've done our share!

COL. HUSSEK. I never thought I'd hear a nephew of mine confess to being a coward! It's the greatest regret of my life that I—

ANNA. Oh, Grandfather, don't excite yourself! You

55

know he doesn't mean it. . . . Uncle Oswald, you mustn't be such a tease!

OSWALD. Well, you don't want Grandpa to be killed, do you? Or even your lazy old Uncle, I hope? Throw me the matches, there's a good girl.

[ANNA *does so.*]

MRS. THORVALD. I think I *will* have a second cup, Martha, after all. I shan't sleep a wink, in any case. . . . Eric, dear, you haven't touched yours. Don't you want it?

ERIC. No, thank you, Mother.

MRS. THORVALD. Well, it *has* been a day of excitements! Those poor, poor children! I shall never dare to go by bus again! I suppose Ostnia will apologize. . . .

DR. THORVALD. They'll have to! The evidence of their guilt is overwhelming.

MARTHA. You can't apologize for murder! They must be punished!

[*Both wireless sets give the time signal.*]

DR. THORVALD. Ssh! The news is coming on!

ANNA [*calling*]. Mother! The news!

WESTLAND RADIO. Maria Kinderheim, the six-year old child injured in the bomb outrage at the Iron Bridge, died in hospital this evening. This brings the number of the Westland dead up to nineteen.

[*Enter* MRS. VRODNY.]

OSTNIAN RADIO. Peter Vollard, the eighty-year-old labourer injured in the bomb outrage at the Iron

Bridge, died in hospital this evening. This brings
the number of the Ostnian dead up to twenty.

Westland Radio. The Minister for Propaganda and
the Minister for Air and Marine flew to Castle Tu-
borg this afternoon to discuss with the Leader
what steps should be taken.... It is rumoured that
the Ostnian Government is calling up the nine-
teen-fourteen and nineteen-fifteen classes.

Ostnian Radio. An emergency meeting of the Cabinet
was called this evening to consider what steps
should be taken.... There are rumours that Westland will order general mobilization.

Westland Radio. In view of the extreme gravity of
the situation ...

Ostnian Radio. In view of the extreme gravity of the
situation ...

Westland Radio. The Leader ...

Ostnian Radio. His Majesty the King ...

Westland Radio. Has decided ...

Ostnian Radio. Has graciously consented ...

Westland Radio. To address the nation ...

Ostnian Radio. To address his people ...

Westland Radio. The address will be broadcast from
all stations at midnight.

Ostnian Radio. The address will be broadcast from all
stations at midnight.

> [*Throughout the scene which follows, the
> two wireless sets provide a background of
> faint, disturbing ominous music.*]

Mrs. Vrodny. When I think of that poor old man who

never did anybody any harm, it makes my blood boil!

[MARTHA *starts collecting the tea things.*]

MRS. THORVALD. The poor mite! She was only a tiny tot!

ANNA. It's horrible! How can anyone have been such a brute!

MRS. VRODNY. All Westlanders are brutes, dear.

ANNA. Some of them were killed, too; weren't they, Mother?

MRS. VRODNY. How do you know? The papers don't say so. The Westlanders are such liars, anyhow!

MRS. THORVALD. The demonstration in the market square was enormous. I could hardly push my way through!

DR. THORVALD. I've never seen the students so moved. We had to suspend all lectures for the day.

MRS. VRODNY. There was a crowd outside Benets' this afternoon. They were smashing the windows.

COL. HUSSEK. Serve them right! We don't want any dirty Westlanders here, cheating us out of our money! Most of them are spies! It's high time we cleared out the lot!

OSWALD. Well, I never did care for Westland much. The women have thick ankles. All the same, I hope they don't sack Freddy from the Long Bar. He mixes the best cocktails in Ostnia.

[*Exit* MARTHA, *with tray.*]

MRS. THORVALD. I met Bob Veigal in the street to-day. Such a nice boy! And quite high up in his

58

shock-troop already. He was so upset. I could hardly get a word out of him except: "We must avenge the Iron Bridge!"

COL. HUSSEK. We must have action! You can't bandy words with murderers! We must avenge the Iron Bridge!

ANNA. I think I'll be going to bed, Mother. I've got rather a headache.

[Re-enter MARTHA.]

MRS. VRODNY. But aren't you going to stay and hear the King?

ANNA. I don't think I will, Mother, if you don't mind. Good night. Good night, Uncle. Good night, Grandpa.

[She hurries out, as if anxious to escape from them all.]

MRS. VRODNY. She's been so quiet all day. I'm afraid she's not well.

MRS. THORVALD. Eric, dear, you're very silent, this evening. Aren't you feeling well?

ERIC [abruptly]. I've got a headache. I'm going to bed.

MARTHA. But Eric, the Leader!

MRS. THORVALD. Oh, Martha! Don't worry him to-night! You can tell him all about it in the morning. [To ERIC.] You'll find some aspirin in the top drawer of my dressing-table.

ERIC. Thanks, Mother. Good night.

[Exit.]

MRS. THORVALD. It must have been a very tiring day for him, with all these demonstrations.

DR. THORVALD. I wonder. . . . I'm not very happy about him, Hilda. I'm afraid he's making some unhealthy friendships. They play at being radicals, pacifists, goodness knows what. Eric's such a child. He doesn't realize what this business means. This crime strikes at the whole basis of European civilization.

MRS. VRODNY. Did you read Father Ambrose's article on the consequences of heresy? We must defend the Church. The Church is in danger!

OSWALD. I was taken to a service in Westland, once. God, I was bored! All those extempore prayers!

MARTHA. The Ostnians aren't civilized! They're savages! They burn incense and worship idols!

> [Noise and singing and the tramp of marching feet off stage. All the characters move excitedly towards their respective windows, COL. HUSSEK propelling himself in his invalid chair. From this moment the acting works up to a note of hysteria.]

MRS. VRODNY [at window]. Look, Father! The Air Force cadets!

MRS. THORVALD [at window]. It's the students! Hundreds of them!

OSWALD. They're tight!

MARTHA. The hour is at hand!

COL. HUSSEK. Stout fellows!

MRS. THORVALD. How happy they look in their uniforms! I wish Eric was among them!

60

[*The two songs which follow should be sung simultaneously.*]

WESTLAND STUDENTS [*off stage, left.*]

Brightly the sun on our weapons is gleaming,
　　Brave is the heart and stout is the arm,
Gone is the night of talking and dreaming,
　　Up and defend your country from harm!

The mountain has strength, the river has beauty,
　　Westland Science, Religion and Art
Inspire us with valour and Westland Duty
　　Echoes in every Westland heart!

Foremost of all the Leader is riding,
　　Love in his bosom and truth on his brow,
Against the whole world in the Leader confiding,
　　Forward to victory follow him now!

OSTNIAN AIR CADETS [*off stage, right*].

Wheel the plane out from its shed,
Though it prove my funeral bed!
I'm so young. No matter, I
Will save my country ere I die!

Hark, I hear the engines roar!
Kiss me, we shall meet no more.
I must fly to north and south.
Kiss me, sweetheart, on the mouth!

Far from Mother, far from crowds,
I must fight among the clouds
Where the searchlights mow the sky,
I must fight and I must die!

DR. THORVALD. It's the spirit of Pericles! The poets have not sung in vain!

MRS. VRODNY. I wish I were a man!

MARTHA. Out of the pit! Out of the mire and clay!

OSWALD. Perhaps I ought to do something!

MRS. THORVALD. The cards did not lie!

COL. HUSSEK. This makes me feel a boy again!

DR. THORVALD. Some people have asked the meaning of history. They have their answer!

MRS. VRODNY. They looked like princes!

MARTHA. The righteous shall inherit the earth!

OSWALD. I shall drink less and less!

MRS. THORVALD. My headache's quite gone!

MRS. VRODNY. We shall be very famous indeed!

MRS. THORVALD. We shall never die!

COL. HUSSEK. I have never lost a battle!

DR. THORVALD. Everything's perfectly clear, now!

OSWALD. After this, we shall all be much richer!

COL. HUSSEK. We are doing splendidly!

MARTHA. God is very glad!

OSTNIAN RADIO. This is Ostnia calling the world!

WESTLAND RADIO. This is Westland calling the world!

OSTNIAN RADIO. His Majesty the King!

WESTLAND RADIO. The Leader!

KING'S VOICE [through radio, right]. It is hard to find words to express . . .

LEADER'S VOICE [through radio, left]. The unceasing struggle of my life has been rewarded . . .

KING. How deeply touched we have been . . .

LEADER. Westland is restored to her greatness . . .

KING. By all the offers of service and sacrifice . . .

LEADER. One heart, one voice, one nation . . .

KING. Which have poured in from every corner of Our country . . .

LEADER. It is a lie to say that Westland has ever stooped to baseness . . .

KING. And from every class of people, even the poorest . . .

LEADER. It is a lie to say that Westland *could* ever stoop to baseness . . .

KING. These last few days of terrible anxiety have brought us all very close together . . .

LEADER. It is a lie to say that Westland wants war . . .

KING. We all, I know, pray from the bottom of our hearts . . .

LEADER. Westland stands in Europe as a great bastion . . .

KING. That this crisis may pass away . . .

LEADER. Against the tide of anarchy . . .

KING. Our Ministers are doing everything in their power . . .

LEADER. Westland lives and Westland soil are sacred . . .

KING. To avoid any irreparable step . . .

LEADER. Should any human power dare to touch either . . .

KING. But should the worst happen . . .

LEADER. It will have to face the holy anger of a nation in arms . . .

KING. We shall face it in a spirit worthy of the great traditions of our fathers . . .

LEADER. That will not sheathe the sword . . .

KING. To whom honour was more precious than life itself . . .

LEADER. Till it has paid for its folly with its blood . . .

KING. We stand before the bar of history . . .

LEADER. For, were Westland to suffer one unrequited wrong . . .

KING. Confident that right must triumph . . .

LEADER. I should have no wish to live!

KING. And we shall endure to the end!

> [*The wireless sets play their respective national anthems.*]

COL. HUSSEK [*standing up in his chair, in great excitement*]. God save the King! God save the King!

> [*He collapses.*]

MRS. VRODNY. Father! [*She runs to him.*] Quick, Oswald, the brandy!

MRS. THORVALD. Dear me, I feel quite exhausted!

OSWALD [*looking in cupboard*]. There's no brandy left. He'll have to have my whisky.

MRS. VRODNY. Hurry!

> [*Oswald gives her the bottle and a glass.*]
> Here, Father! [*Gives Hussek a sip.*] Take this.

DR. THORVALD. Time we all went to bed. There won't be any more news tonight. Come along, Hilda.

COL. HUSSEK [*faintly, opening his eyes*]. Thank you, my dear . . . Sorry . . . my heart, again . . . Better now . . . It's been a great day . . .

MRS. VRODNY. [*to Oswald*]. Help me to get him to bed.

MRS. THORVALD. You're not staying up, are you, Martha dear?

MARTHA. I'll follow you in a minute.

OSWALD [*pushing the* COLONEL's *chair*]. Up we go!

[*Exeunt* DR. *and* MRS. THORVALD.]

Feeling better now? That whisky's wonderful stuff!

[*Exeunt* OSWALD *and* COLONEL, *followed by* MRS. VRODNY *who turns out the light, so that the right of the stage is darkened.*]

MARTHA [*kneeling before the* LEADER's *portrait*]. My hero! My Leader! You will fight them, won't you? Say you will! Say you will! [*Kneels for a moment, then rises, salutes and exits, turning out light.*]

[*The whole stage is now in complete darkness for some moments. Distant, dreamy music, off stage. Then a spotlight illuminates a small area in the middle of the stage. The various chairs and tables should have been pushed back, so that they are visible only as indistinct shapes in the surrounding darkness. Enter* ERIC *and* ANNA, *left and right respectively. They advance slowly, like sleep-walkers, until they stand just outside the circle of light, facing each other.*]

ERIC. Is that you, Anna?

ANNA. Yes, Eric.

[*They both take a step forward into the light-circle.*]

ERIC. I knew I could make this happen!

ANNA. Where are we?

ERIC. In the place that I have found for us,
    The place that I have hoped for since I was born,
    Born, as we all are, into a world full of fear,
    Where the faces are not the faces of the happy,
    Where the disappointed hate the young
    And the disinherited weep in vain.
    Not that any are wanting this world, any;
    The truckdriver, the executive setting his watch,
    The clerk entraining for the office, us,
    All of us wishing always it were different.
    All of us wanting to be kind and honest,
    Good neighbours and good parents and good chil-
        dren,
    To be beautiful and likable and happy.
    Ever since I was born I have been looking,
    Looking for a place where I could really be myself,
    For a person who would see me as I really am.
    And I have found them both, found them now,
        found them here.
    This is the good place.
ANNA. I am afraid. The darkness is so near.
ERIC. This is the good place
    Where the air is not filled with screams of hatred
    Nor words of great and good men twisted
    To flatter conceit and justify murder.
    Here are no family quarrels or public meetings,
    No disease or old age. No death.
    Here we can be really alone,
    Alone with our love, our faith, our knowledge.
    I've struggled for this ever since I saw you.

66

A long time, Anna. Did you know that?

ANNA. A long time, Eric, yes, I've felt you near me.
You took my arm in crowded shops,
Helping me choose.
Behind my chair as I sat sewing, you stood
And gave me patience. Often you sat
Beside me in the park and told me stories
Of couples in the panting unfair city
Who loved each other all their lives.
Oh, when I went to dances, all my partners
Were you, were you.

ERIC. Ever since I remember I've caught glimpses of
you,
At first, far off, a nature on the crag,
Far off down the long poplar avenue, a traveller.
I've seen your face reflected in the river
As I sat fishing; and when I read a book
Your face would come between me and the print
Like an ambition, nearer and clearer every day.
And now, at last . . .

ANNA. Do They see, too?

ERIC. They do not want to see. Their blindness is
Their pride, their constitution and their town
Where Love and Truth are movements under-
ground,
Dreading arrest and torture.

ANNA. Oh, Eric, I'm so afraid of them!

ERIC. Locked in each other's arms, we form a tower
They cannot shake or enter. Our love
Is the far and unsuspected island

Their prestige does not hold.

ANNA. I wish that this could last for ever.

ERIC. It can, Anna, it can! Nothing matters now
But you and I. This is the everlasting garden
Where we shall walk together always,
Happy, happy, happy, happy.

ANNA. You do not know their power. They know,
know all.
They let us meet but only to torment us
When they have proved our guilt. They grin be-
hind our joy,
Waiting their time. Oh, if we take one step
Towards our love, the grace will vanish,
Our peace smash like a vase. Oh, we shall see
The threatening faces sudden at the window, hear
The furious knocking on the door,
The cry of anger from the high-backed chair.

ERIC. It can't be true! It shan't be true!
Our love is stronger than their hate!
Kiss me.

ANNA. Don't, don't! You'll make them angry!
We shall be punished!

ERIC. I don't care! I defy them!

[*He steps forward to embrace her. The stage
is immediately plunged in darkness. Their
voices now begin to grow fainter.*]

VOICES. [*These should be taken by the actors playing
DR. THORVALD and MRS. VRODNY, and should
have the resonant disembodied quality of an echo*].
NO!

68

ERIC'S VOICE. Anna, Anna. Where are you?

ANNA'S VOICE. Where are you, Eric?

ERIC. Come back.

ANNA. I can't. They're too strong. Help me, Eric. They're taking me away.

VOICE 1. Take her away.

ERIC. They're holding me back.

VOICE 2. Hold him back.

ANNA. I shall never see you again.

BOTH VOICES. Never see $\begin{Bmatrix} \text{him} \\ \text{her} \end{Bmatrix}$ again.

ERIC. Anna. Can you hear me? I swear I'll come back to you. I'll beat them somehow. Only wait for me, Anna. Promise you'll wait.

ANNA. I promise, Eric.

VOICE 2 [whispering]. Tradition and breeding count.

VOICE 1 [whispering]. You can't wipe out the history of a thousand years.

CURTAIN

[*BEFORE THE CURTAIN*]

[*Five men, three women. Three couples are waltzing. The two remaining men, who are supposed to be left-wing political workers, are watching, in the background.*]

FIRST MALE DANCER.

> The papers say there'll be war before long;
> Sometimes they're right, and sometimes they're
>> wrong.

SECOND MALE DANCER.

> There's a lot of talk in a wireless set
> And a lot more promised than you'll ever get.

FIRST LEFTIST.

> Don't believe them,
> Only fools let words deceive them.
> Resist the snare, the scare
> Of something that's not really there.
> These voices commit treason
> Against all truth and reason,
> Using an unreal aggression
> To blind you to your real oppression;
> Truth is elsewhere.
> Understand the motive, penetrate the lie
> Or you will die.

THIRD MALE DANCER.

> The Winter comes, the Summer goes;
> If there's a war, we shall fight, I suppose.

FIRST MALE DANCER.

> The larder is cold, the kitchen is hot;
> If we go we'll be killed, if we don't we'll be shot.

SECOND LEFTIST.

> What they can do depends on you,
> You are many, they are few,
> Afraid for their trade, afraid
> Of the overworked and the underpaid.
> Do not go; they know
> That though they seem so strong
> Their power lasts so long
> As you are undecided and divided;
> Understand the wrong;
> Understand the fact;
> Unite and act.

SECOND MALE DANCER.

> There're hills in the north and sea in the south;
> It's wiser not to open your mouth.

THIRD MALE DANCER.

> Soldiers have guns and are used in attack;
> More of them go than ever come back.

FIRST FEMALE DANCER.

> What shall I say to the child at my knee
> When you fall in the mountains or sink in the sea?

SECOND FEMALE DANCER.

> What shall we do if you lose a leg?
> Sing for our supper, or steal or beg?

FIRST LEFTIST.

> It's weak to submit,
> Then cry when you are hit.
> It's mad to die
> For what you know to be a lie.
> And whom you kill
> Depends upon your will.
> Their blood is upon your head.
> Choose to live.
> The dead cannot forgive
> Nor will time pardon the dead.

THIRD FEMALE DANCER.

> What is a parlour, what is a bed
> But a place to weep in when you are dead?

FIRST MALE DANCER.

> It's good-bye to the bench and good-bye to the
> wife
> And good-bye for good to somebody's life.

SECOND MALE DANCER.

> Our country's in danger, and our cause is just;
> If no one's mistaken, it's conquer or bust.

SECOND LEFTIST.

> The country is in danger
> But not from any stranger.
> Your enemies are here
> Whom you should fight, not fear,
> For till they cease
> The earth will know no peace.
> Learn to know
> Your friend from your foe.

THIRD MALE DANCER.
>   But if some one's mistaken or lying or mad,
>   Or if we're defeated, it will be just too bad.

BLACK OUT

ACT TWO

SCENE II

[VALERIAN's *study. Just after midnight.*]

> [VALERIAN *and* STAHL, *with brandy glasses before them, are listening to the* LEADER'S *speech on the radio.*]

LEADER'S VOICE. . . . it will have to face the holy anger of a nation in arms, that will not sheathe the sword till it has paid for its folly with its blood. For, were Westland to suffer one unrequited wrong, I should have no wish to live!

VALERIAN. Admirable sentiments! A little more brandy, my dear Stahl?

STAHL. Thanks. . . . I need it. . . . [*Pours and drinks.*] The man's got a voice like a corncrake!

VALERIAN. Oh, I can't agree with you there! His delivery is really excellent. He has mastered all the tricks. I'm told that he once took lessons from Sacha Guitry.

STAHL. I didn't like the tone of that speech at all. . . . You know he saw the General Staff again, this evening? You mark my words, this is to prepare the

75

country for mobilization. The decree's probably signed already.

VALERIAN. Hammel would never agree to it.

STAHL. Then he'll override Hammel. We're dealing with a madman. You said so yourself.

VALERIAN. Very well. Let us suppose that mobilization is ordered. What does that mean, nowadays? Nothing! We live in an age of bluff. The boys shout until they are hoarse, and the politicians hunt for a formula under the conference-table. A lot of noise to cover up an enormous cold funk.

STAHL. Cold funk is an exceedingly dangerous state of mind. A coward often hits first.

VALERIAN. But, I ask you, who wants war? Certainly not the industrialists; the arms race is good for another five years at least. Certainly not the politicians; they're far too jealous of the military and afraid of losing their jobs. Even the General Staffs don't want it; they're both perfectly happy playing at mechanization. . . . Do you seriously imagine that wars nowadays are caused by some escaped lunatic putting a bomb under a bridge and blowing up an omnibus? There have been worse provocations in the past, and there will be worse in the future. The national honour will swallow them all quite conveniently. It has a very strong digestion.

[Enter LESSEP, with papers.]

LESSEP. Here are the latest press bulletins, Mr. Valerian.

VALERIAN. Thank you.

[Reads. Exit LESSEP.]

76

STAHL. Anything fresh?

VALERIAN. Nothing. Students' demonstrations. Patriotic speeches. All the customary nonsense. . . . Our operatives gathered outside the Villa Kismet during the lunch hour and cheered the Leader till it was time to go back to work. Then two of the organizers of the illegal trades union were recognized in the crowd, and so roughly handled that the Police had to take them into preventive custody. . . . The Iron Bridge incident has certainly solved some of our labour problems—for the moment.

STAHL. Yes—for the moment. . . . But, even supposing that there's no war, how will all this end?

VALERIAN. It will end itself. In ten days there will be a new distraction—an international football match or a girl found murdered in her bath. . . . [Reads.] This is rather amusing. An Ostnian journalist has written an article proving conclusively that the Iron Bridge bomb was fired by order of myself!

STAHL. Haha! Thank goodness for something to laugh at, anyway!

VALERIAN. "The sinister Westland industrialists, realizing that they have brought their country to the verge of ruin, attempt a desperate gambler's throw . . ." You know Stahl, a crime of this sort— so pointless, so entirely without motive—is bound to have a curious psychological effect upon everybody. Don't you sometimes wake up in the night, and wonder: Who did it? Like the reader of a detective story? And, of course, the most apparently

77

innocent are the most suspect. Perhaps it was the Ostnian archbishop. Perhaps it was the wife of our municipal librarian. Perhaps it was my butler, Manners. And then, inevitably, one begins to wonder: was it I myself, in a moment of insanity, followed by amnesia? Have I an alibi? Ought I to go to the police and confess? Madness is so infectious.

STAHL. In your list of suspects, you've forgotten the chief madman. Why shouldn't it have been the Leader, himself?

VALERIAN. Ah, no, my friend. The Leader is the only man in all Westland who is quite above suspicion. If he had done it, he would never have been able to resist telling us so! [*Listening.*] I wonder who that is on the stairs? Surely it can't be a visitor, at this hour of the night?

[*Enter* MANNERS.]

MANNERS. It's the Leader, sir.

STAHL. Gracious! I'd better clear out.

VALERIAN. No. Please stay. This will be interesting.

[*Enter the* LEADER *and Storm-Trooper* GRIMM, *right. The* LEADER's *whole manner has changed. He is obviously exhausted. He speaks gently, almost timidly. Storm-Trooper* GRIMM *takes up his position at the back of the stage. Throughout the scene which follows, he neither moves nor speaks.*]

LEADER. May I come in?

VALERIAN. This is an unexpected honour.

LEADER. I saw your light in the window, on my way back from the broadcasting station.

VALERIAN. We have been listening to your speech.

LEADER [*sinking into a chair*]. How quiet it is in here! All day long I have been surrounded by shouting, noise, crowds. I thought: for a few moments I shall be able to be quiet. . . .

STAHL. Perhaps, my Leader, you'd prefer to be left alone?

LEADER. No, no. I hate to be alone. Don't leave me, any of you. . . .

VALERIAN. You must be very tired?

LEADER. More tired than I have ever been in my whole life.

VALERIAN. You'll take some wine? Something to eat?
[*The* LEADER *does not reply.* VALERIAN *makes a sign to* MANNERS, *who goes out.*]

LEADER [*begins to speak quietly, then with rising hysteria*]. For five nights I have lain awake, wondering: What shall I do? What shall I do? And no one can decide for me. No one! I alone must make the final choice. Peace or war? It is a terrible burden to put upon the shoulders of one man. . . . You think I am strong? No, I am weak, weak. . . . I never wished to be the Leader. It was forced upon me. Forced upon me, I tell you, by the men who said they were my friends, and who thought only of their own ambition. They made use of me. They made use of my love for my dear country. They never loved West-land as I did. . . . I stood on a platform in a village

79

hall or a table in a little restaurant—when I began to speak, people listened. More and more people. It was like a dream. I was proud of my power. They flattered me. . . . And I was so simple; only a poor out-of-work bank-clerk. I believed them. . . . My parents were country people. They gave their last savings to have me educated. "You mustn't grow up to be a peasant," they told me. And I obeyed them. I worked hard. I would have been contented with so little. I was afraid of the world, of the rich people in their fine houses. I feared them and I hated them. . . . And then I found that I could speak. It was easy. So easy. I had money, friends. They told me: "You will be a great man." I learnt their ways. Step by step. Climbing higher and higher. I had to be cunning. I had to do horrible things. I had to intrigue and murder. Nobody knows that I did it all for Westland. *Only* for Westland. . . . Don't you believe me?

VALERIAN [*soothingly*]. Certainly we believe you.

LEADER. In the nights, when my people are all asleep, I lie and tremble. You would never understand. . . . It's like some terrible nightmare. I—I alone, am responsible. And at the great receptions, when I stand there in my uniform, with all the foreign diplomats and the beautiful well-born women around me (the women I used to dream of when I was a poor boy in an office), I want to scream in all their faces: "Leave me alone! Leave me alone! Let me go back to my parents' cottage! Let me be humble and free!" Some of these women know what I am feeling. I see it in their eyes. How they despise me! [*Screaming.*] Don't you see how you are all torturing me? I can't bear it! I must bear it! I can't bear it! [*Covers his face with his hands and sobs.*] No! No! No! No!

> [VALERIAN *goes quietly over to the gramophone, and starts the record of Rameau's Tambourin. Then he and* STAHL *remain motionless, watching the* LEADER. *During the music,* MANNERS *comes in, silently places a tray of cold supper near the* LEADER'S *chair, and exits.*]

> [*As the music proceeds, the* LEADER'S *sobbing quietens and stops. For some time he remains motionless, his face in his hands. Then, slowly, he raises his head. His expression is now calm and radiant. When the music stops, he is smiling.*]

LEADER. Ah . . . that music! How clearly I see the way now! [*Rising to his feet.*] Listen, all of you. I have made a great decision! Tomorrow morning, the whole world will hear that I have withdrawn the Westland troops, unconditionally, ten miles from the frontier. It will hear that I have proposed to Ostnia a pact of non-aggression, guaranteeing the sanctity of the frontier for a thousand years!

STAHL. My Leader, may I congratulate you? This is the finest thing you have ever done!

LEADER. They will not sneer at me any more, will they,

in England and France and America? They will
not be able to say I wanted war. My decision will
be famous. It will be praised in the history books.
I will make my country the greatest of all gifts—
the gift of peace!

STAHL. This is magnificent!

LEADER. Tomorrow night you will hear my greatest
speech. My Peace Speech. I shall stand before my
shock troopers and I shall tell them: War is glorious, but Peace is more glorious still! And I shall
convince them! I know it! I am strong, now! They
may not understand at first, but they will obey,
because it is my will. The will of their Leader. The
immutable, unconquerable will of the Westland
nation. . . . I must speak to General Staff Headquarters, at once!

STAHL [aside]. Valerian, you have saved us all!

VALERIAN [aside]. I receive your thanks on behalf of
poor Rameau. If only he were alive! How very surprised he would be!

[Enter LESSEP, with envelope.]

LESSEP. My Leader, an urgent despatch from General
Staff Headquarters.

LEADER [reads, crumples paper. Furiously]. They have
dared! You will bear witness, all of you, that Westland had no hand in this! You will record my decision for the judgment of posterity!

STAHL. But—my Leader, what has happened?

LEADER. An hour ago, the Ostnian troops crossed our
frontier! Kapra has been bombed by Ostnian

planes. Women and children foully, heartlessly murdered!

STAHL. Oh, my God!

VALERIAN. The idiots!

LEADER. The die is cast! The name of Ostnia shall be blotted from the map of Europe for ever!

STAHL. This is the end of everything!

LEADER [*in his platform manner*]. Confident in the justice of our cause, and determined to defend our sacred Westland homesteads to the last, we swear—

[*He is still shouting as the* CURTAIN *falls*]

ACT THREE

ACT THREE

SCENE I

[*The Ostnia-Westland Room. It is early evening. On the left of stage, MARTHA sits rolling bandages. MRS. THORVALD is knitting a muffler, DR. THORVALD is reading the casualty lists in the newspaper.*]

[*On the right of the stage sits MRS. VRODNY, all in black, alone. She is staring in front of her, with a fixed expression. She looks much older.*]

[*It is noticeable that both homes seem shabbier and poorer than in the earlier scenes. Several pieces of furniture are missing. Indeed, the VRODNY-HUSSEK home is almost bare.*]

MRS. THORVALD. Mrs. Veigal says it was perfectly wonderful. She could hear Bob's voice just as if he were in the room. He told her not to worry. Those who have passed over are all very happy. He said the Other Side was difficult to describe, but it was like listening to glorious music!

MARTHA. It's wicked, Hilda; and dangerous as well! How does she know she wasn't talking to an evil spirit?

MRS. THORVALD. I don't see that it can do any harm.

And it's such a comfort to her! Poor woman, she idolized Bob!

DR. THORVALD. Well, at least she can be proud of him! Listen to this: "Robert Veigal. Killed in action. December the tenth. The Blue Order. For conspicuous gallantry in the face of the enemy." The casualty lists this evening are terrible! That offensive on the Slype Canal was a shambles. If they don't make some big changes on the General Staff soon, there'll be trouble! Hammel ought to have been retired years ago.

MARTHA. There're too many healthy young men slacking in cushy staff jobs! As for those cowardly pacifists, I can't think why they're allowed to have a soft time in prison! They ought to be sent to the firing-line!

MRS. THORVALD. Oh, Martha, you're cruel! After all, Eric's your nephew!

DR. THORVALD. Hilda, I've told you before never to mention his name in this house again! The shame of it has almost killed me!

MRS. THORVALD. I suppose you wish he'd been blown to pieces by a shell, like Bob Veigal! Well, perhaps he *is* dead! They wouldn't tell me anything!

DR. THORVALD. You didn't go to the prison?

MRS. THORVALD. Yes I did! So there! He's my son and I want to see him! I don't care about anything, any more. . . . Eric, my darling boy, what have they done to you?

[*She bursts into tears.*]

DR. THORVALD. She's overwrought. She doesn't know what she's saying. . . . Martha, could you make some coffee? It would do her good.

MARTHA. We haven't any coffee. And we've used up our week's ration of sugar, already. There isn't any more firewood, either.

DR. THORVALD. I suppose we shall have to burn another of the spare-room chairs. [*With an attempt to smile.*] Soon we shall be sitting on the floor!

MARTHA. I'll see what I can find.

[*Exits.*]

DR. THORVALD [*rising and going over to his wife*]. I'm sorry, dear!

MRS. THORVALD [*sobbing*]. You're not! You don't love Eric! You never did!

DR. THORVALD. Perhaps I have been rather harsh. I haven't tried to understand what made him act as he did. You see, I was brought up to think that a man's greatest privilege was to fight for his country; and it's hard to change one's ideas. Perhaps we were all wrong. War seems so beastly when it actually happens! Perhaps "country" and "frontier" are old-fashioned words that don't mean anything now. What are we really fighting for? I feel so muddled! It's not so easy to rearrange one's beliefs, at our age. For we're both getting on, aren't we, dear? You must help me. We've got no one to turn to now, but each other. We must try to think of all the happy times we've had together. . . . You remember them too, don't you, Hilda? We must

89

make a new start. . . . I tell you what I'll do—to-morrow I'll go down to the prison myself! Perhaps I shall be able to get something out of them!

Mrs. Thorvald [*looks up and smiles*]. Thank you, dear!

Dr. Thorvald. That's better! Give me a kiss! [*They embrace and remain seated together, holding hands.*] This is quite like old times, isn't it?

[*Enter Anna, also in black.*]

Mrs. Vrodny [*without turning her head, in a harsh, croaking voice*]. How much did he give you?

Anna. Eight hundred and fifty.

Mrs. Vrodny. That's ridiculous! It cost twelve hundred!

Anna. Oh, Mother, I know! I argued and argued with him! But it was no use. He just laughed. I was so afraid he might refuse to take it at all. Then he tried to kiss me. . . . It was beastly!

Mrs. Vrodny. Your father gave me that brooch on our engagement-day.

Anna. Why did you do it, Mother? Wasn't there anything else?

Mrs. Vrodny. It was the last I had. But what does it matter?

Anna. You're worn out. Why don't you take a day in bed? I'll look after everything.

Mrs. Vrodny. Nonsense! You've got your hospital work to do. Aren't you on night duty this week? You ought to be getting your things on now.

Anna. Very well, Mother.

[*Exit, right.*]

[*Enter* MARTHA, *with tray, left.*]

MARTHA. I've made you some herbal tea. It's all there is.

MRS. THORVALD. How sweet of you, Martha! [*To* DR. THORVALD.] I haven't had time to look at the paper yet. Is there any real news? They never tell us anything!

DR. THORVALD. Nothing much. All the fronts were quiet, this morning. The usual rumours of desertion and mutinies in the Ostnian regiments. Probably nonsense. But there seems no doubt that they're having a very bad time with the plague. They're dying by thousands, apparently!

MARTHA. It shows there's some justice in the world!

MRS. THORVALD [*notices that there are only two cups on the tray*]. Won't you have a cup as well, Martha? You're not looking too grand, you know. Are you all right?

MARTHA. I've got a bad headache, that's all. I think perhaps a cup would do me good. I'm feeling so thirsty!

[*Exits.*]

DR. THORVALD. Of course, the papers have censored it, but I hear that there've been one or two cases here, among the prisoners of war.

MRS. THORVALD. Oliver! How dreadful! Supposing it spreads!

DR. THORVALD. Oh, we're safe enough!

MRS. THORVALD. But just suppose it does! What are the symptoms?

DR. THORVALD. I don't know exactly. A swelling under

the arm, I believe. . . . But you mustn't worry your head about that!

[*Enter* Anna, *in nurse's uniform.*]

Anna. I'm off now, Mother.

Mrs. Vrodny. Keep clear of the office when you go downstairs. They took away the caretaker, this morning.

Anna [*hysterically*]. Can't they do anything to stop it, before it kills everybody in the whole world? It's taken Grandfather. It's taken Uncle Oswald. It'll take us, too, soon! What have we all done that we should be destroyed like this? Nobody's *alive* any more! I look at the faces in the streets, and they're not the faces of living people! We're all dead!

Mrs. Vrodny. Anna! Control yourself!

[*As in Act Two, Scene I, the sound of marching feet is heard. But this time there is no music, only the tap of a drum.*]

[Anna *goes to window. Enter* Martha, *with her cup.*]

Mrs. Thorvald. Those horrible drums! Oh, shut the window! I can't bear the sound any more!

Dr. Thorvald [*going to window*]. They're mere boys! How many of them will be alive in a week's time? They used to sing once. . . . Oh, God, why can't it stop!

[*Bangs down window.*]

Mrs. Vrodny. Listen to them marching! Think what those men are going to face. Grandfather was a soldier, and his father before him. We're the only

ones left now. Perhaps we shan't be here much
longer. But remember that, whatever happens to
you, you come of a family of soldiers! Never forget
that!

[*The marching dies away.*]

DR. THORVALD. I must be off to the university. We're
working out a new scheme of courses for the blind.
Can I get anything for you in town?

MARTHA. Could you get me some liniment?

MRS. THORVALD. Liniment? What for, Martha? Have
you hurt yourself?

MARTHA. I don't know. I've got such a funny swelling.

DR. THORVALD [*exchanging a quick glance with his
wife.*] A swelling?

MRS. THORVALD. How long have you had it?

MARTHA. Only since this morning. It came up quite
suddenly.

DR. THORVALD. Could you have bruised yourself, somehow?

MARTHA. Oh no, I'm quite sure I haven't. . . . But it
hurts!

DR. THORVALD [*trying to speak calmly*]. Where, exactly, is this swelling, Martha?

MARTHA. Here. Under my arm. . . . Why, what's the
matter?

MRS. THORVALD [*jumping up with a scream*]. She's got
it! She's got the plague! Don't let her touch me!
Keep her away! We shall catch it! We shall all die!

DR. THORVALD. Quiet, Hilda! I don't expect it's anything serious, but you'd better go to your room,

Martha . . . . I'll phone for the doctor at once!

> [*He and his wife instinctively back away from* MARTHA *into a corner of the stage.*]

MARTHA [*hysterical*]. No! No! It can't be! I won't! I've been good! You can't let me die! I've never had a chance! You don't know how I've suffered! You don't know what it's like to be ugly, to see everyone else getting married, to spend your life looking after other people's children! I've sacrificed everything! I had brains! I might have had a brilliant career, but I gave it all up for you! I've been more loyal than any of them! If you let me die, there's no point in being good, any more! It doesn't matter! It's all a lie! I've never been happy! I've been betrayed!

ANNA [*as if listening to sounds in the very far distance*] Mother . . . can't you hear them, over there? They're crying, they're suffering—just like us!

MRS. VRODNY [*speaking with a kind of terrible obstinacy, which belies her words*]. I hear nothing!

MARTHA [*runs to the* LEADER'S *portrait.*] Oh, my Leader! Say you don't mean it! Say I'm going to live! Speak to me!

> [*She falls on her knees before the picture, and, in doing so, switches on the wireless.*]

WESTLAND RADIO [*tonelessly, like a time-signal*]. Kill, Kill, Kill, Kill, Kill! [*Continues to the end of scene.*]

ANNA [*with an involuntary despairing cry*]. Eric, where are you?

CURTAIN

(BEFORE THE CURTAIN)

[*Three Westland soldiers are grouped behind some kind of simplified construction to represent a parapet. They stare across the stage into the darkness, where the Ostnian trenches are supposed to lie. The Ostnians remain invisible, throughout, but their voices are represented by the two remaining male members of the chorus, off stage. One of the Westland soldiers has an accordion, to which he sings:*]

FIRST SOLDIER.

> Ben was a four foot seven Wop,
> He worked all night in a bucket-shop
> On cocoa, and sandwiches,
> And bathed on Sunday evenings.

> In winter when the woods were bare
> He walked to work in his underwear
> With his hat in his hand,
> But his watch was broken.

> He met his Chief in the Underground,
> He bit him hard till he turned round
> In the neck, and the ear,
> And the left-hand bottom corner.

> He loved his wife though she was cruel,
> He gave her an imitation jewel

> In a box, a black eye,
> And a very small packet of Woodbines.

OSTNIAN [*off stage*]. The *only* brand!

SECOND SOLDIER. Ssh! Did you hear that?

FIRST SOLDIER. The bleeders! I'll show 'em. [*Picks up rifle.*]

THIRD SOLDIER. Sit down, yer fool. You'll start something. [*Shouts across stage.*] Hullo!

OSTNIAN [*off stage*]. Hullo!

THIRD SOLDIER. Wot's it like, your side?

OSTNIAN [*off stage*]. Wet.

THIRD SOLDIER. Same here.

OSTNIAN [*off stage*]. Got any cigarettes?

SECOND SOLDIER. Yes. But no ruddy matches.

OSTNIAN. [*off stage*]. We've got matches. Swop?

SECOND SOLDIER. Right. Coming over. [*Throws matches.*]

OSTNIAN [*off stage*]. Thanks. Coming over. [*The packet of cigarettes flies out of the darkness but falls short, outside the parapet.*] Sorry!

FIRST SOLDIER. Christ, you Ostnians throw like a pack of school-girls! [*To the others.*] Wait a mo. Gimme a torch.

SECOND SOLDIER. Take care!

FIRST SOLDIER. Oh, they're all right! [*Climbs over parapet and looks for cigarettes.*]

OSTNIAN [*off stage*]. More to the left. Further. There, man! Right under your nose!

FIRST SOLDIER. Got 'em. Thanks, boys. [*Picks up packet and climbs back.*]

OSTNIAN [*singing off stage*].

>What are we fighting for?
>What are we fighting for?

THIRD SOLDIER [*joining in*]. Only the sergeant knows.
[*To* FIRST SOLDIER.] Come on, Angel. Get yer
squeeze-box.

>[FIRST SOLDIER *begins to play the accordion.
Air: "Mademoiselle from Armentiers." The
three Westland soldiers sing the first six verses
in turn, all joining in the chorus.*]

The biscuits are hard and the beef is high,
The weather is wet and the drinks are dry,
We sit in the mud and wonder why.

With faces washed until they shine
The G.H.Q. sit down to dine
A hundred miles behind the line.

The Colonel said he was having a doze;
I looked through the window; a rambler rose
Climbed up his knee in her underclothes.

The chaplain paid us a visit one day,
A shell came to call from over the way,
You should have heard the bastard pray!

The subaltern's heart was full of fire,
Now he hangs on the old barbed wire
All blown up like a motor-tyre.

The sergeant-major gave us hell.
A bullet struck him and he fell.
Where did it come from? Who can tell?

[*The* OSTNIANS *now join in.* OSTNIANS and
WESTLANDERS *sing the following six verses
alternately, joining in the last.*]

Kurt went sick with a pain in his head,
Malingering, the doctor said.
Gave him a pill. Next day he was dead.

Fritz was careless, I'm afraid.
He lost his heart to a parlour-maid.
Now he's lost his head to a hand-grenade.

Karl married a girl with big blue eyes.
He went back on leave; to his surprise
The hat in the hall was not his size.

Oh, No Man's Land is a pleasant place,
You can lie there as long as you lie on your face
Till your uniform is an utter disgrace.

I'd rather eat turkey than humble pie,
I'd rather see mother than lose an eye,
I'd rather kiss a girl than die.

We're sick of the rain and the lice and the smell,
We're sick of the noise of shot and shell,
And the whole bloody war can go to hell!

BLACK OUT

ACT THREE

SCENE II

[VALERIAN's *study.* VALERIAN *is nervously pacing the room.* LESSEP *is seated by the desk, at the telephone. It is night.*]

VALERIAN. Call the hospital again. There must be some news by now!

LESSEP [*dials and speaks into phone*]. Hullo. . . . Is that the Central Hospital? Mr. Valerian wishes to enquire for his butler, Mr. Manners. . . . Thank you. . . .

VALERIAN. I told him not to go into the city; and he disobeyed me—for the first time! He risked his life, Lessep: and do you know why? To try and find me a pot of caviare! Ridiculous, isn't it? [*Going to window.*] Tell me, is the plague really so bad, down there?

LESSEP. It's much worse than they admit. The newspapers are still ordered to minimize it; and they're burying all the dead by night.

VALERIAN. Extraordinary. . . . Up here, we inhabit another world!

LESSEP. But, Mr. Valerian, there's always the danger of infection. Even for us! Forgive my speaking of it

99

again, but don't you think it would be wiser to move? You could go to your villa at Konia. . . .

VALERIAN. If you are frightened you have my permission to go there—alone.

LESSEP. Of course, I'm only thinking of your safety. . . . [*Into telephone.*] Yes? Yes . . . Oh . . . I am very sorry. . . . Thank you. . . .

VALERIAN. Well, what do they say?

LESSEP. Manners . . . I'm afraid he's dead. . . . Half an hour ago. The fever didn't break.

VALERIAN. Dead. . . . So. . . . I'm sorry. . . . Well, there's nothing I can do about it now. [*To LESSEP.*] Have any more reports come in?

LESSEP. Only a telegram from the Tarnberg Colliery. The eight o'clock shift refused to go down, and are threatening to destroy the plant. The manager doesn't think the police are reliable.

VALERIAN. Nothing from Headquarters?

LESSEP. There's been no news of any kind from the front all day. The storm must have broken down the wires. [*Buzzer on desk sounds.*]

VALERIAN. See who that is.

LESSEP. [*into the house telephone*]. Hullo. Speaking. Yes, Mr. Valerian is here.

VALERIAN. Who is it?

LESSEP. It's Mr. Stahl. He's coming upstairs now.

> [*Enter* STAHL. *He is haggard and exhausted. His clothes and raincoat are splashed with mud.*]

STAHL. Valerian! Thank God you're safe!

VALERIAN. My dear Stahl, this is a pleasant surprise. I thought you were visiting our gallant boys in the trenches. Oh dear, where *did* you get that cap? It makes you look like a racing tout. And you're wet through. What have you been doing? How did you get here?

STAHL. I managed to find the airfield. Thank God, most of the pilots are still loyal. We landed in the meadows, a couple of miles from the house. In the pitch darkness. . . . We were lucky not to crash.

VALERIAN. What a state you're in! Lessep, the brandy.

STAHL. Thanks. . . . [*Drinks.*] I'm quite exhausted. Ran most of the way through woods, over ploughed fields . . . didn't dare show myself on the road. . . .

VALERIAN. I say, Stahl, are you tight? What *is* the matter?

STAHL. You mean, you don't know?

VALERIAN. There's been no news all day. The telegraph wires are down.

STAHL. Cut, you mean. . . . When we were only a few miles from the front the car was stopped by a couple of private soldiers, we were told to get out, and taken along to a sort of barn. They wouldn't answer any questions, but there were a lot of officers in the barn, prisoners like myself, and I soon learnt what was happening. The whole Northern sector has mutinied and are fraternizing with the enemy. All officers who tried to stop them were shot out of hand. Jansen was bayoneted in his own headquarters. . . . And that's not all. There was a revolution in the Ostnian capital this morning. The King's hiding somewhere in the mountains; tomorrow he will have abdicated, if he's alive. The Ostnians have got loud-speakers in the front line, calling on their soldiers to make an armistice and revolt against their own government!

VALERIAN. Excellent! Nothing could be better. The new Ostnian government is certain to be incompetent and full of intrigue. It will be our big chance to finish things off. But I'm interrupting you. How did you get away?

STAHL. I managed to bribe one of the guards with a cigarette case.

VALERIAN. Not the one your wife gave you for a silver wedding present? My word, you'll catch it!

STAHL. Valerian, this isn't funny. This humour of yours is becoming a pose. We've got to get out of here. There's nothing either of us can do.

VALERIAN. And where do you propose that we should go?

STAHL. You know I had a cable the other day from Quinta in Rio, asking me to help him build up the South American Trusts? I'm going to accept his offer, and I want you to come too. We need you, Valerian.

VALERIAN. My dear friend, I am too old for carpet-bagging. Quinta would impose his own conditions. He'd use us like office boys.

STAHL. This is no time for false pride. Do you realize,

man, that if you stay here you'll see your life-work ruined before your eyes?

VALERIAN. Steady, steady. Don't get hysterical. Listen, what you tell me doesn't surprise me in the least. I only wonder it hasn't happened before. What can you expect? The war should have been over in three weeks if our friend Hammel had the brains of a fifth-rate actor. It's gone on for nine months. The plague was bad luck certainly, but if our public health authorities had ever learnt to cooperate with each other, it could have been kept within bounds. Of course, there're mutinies and strikes; there'll be more before we're done. There were plenty in the Great War. . . . A lot of people will have to be arrested, and a few of them shot. The Leader will visit the trenches again in person. There'll be an advance of a hundred yards somewhere, the papers will predict an immediate victory, and the workers and the soldiers will go back to their jobs. As for Ostnia. . . .

STAHL. You don't understand. You don't want to. You're crazy with conceit! It wasn't just a little local trouble I saw. The officers told me that only Frommer's 18th route army is still completely loyal. I tell you, it means civil war!

VALERIAN. Very well. Suppose it does. Do you seriously think that a rabble of half-baked townees and farm labourers without any officers can stand up against Frommer, who is certainly the best general we've got? I'm afraid they'll be sorry they were ever born.

Frommer's not a kind old gentleman, and has rather old-fashioned ideas about the sanctity of private property.

STAHL. It's no use arguing. I know what I saw. They tore the tabs off a colonel and shot him in the stomach before my eyes. It was horrible. This is the end.

VALERIAN. If you think so, then it's no good my talking, is it? I'm sorry that our long partnership should come to such a sudden conclusion.

STAHL. But what are you going to do?

VALERIAN. What should I do? Stay here, of course.

LESSEP. Mr. Valerian—what's the use? I beg you to go

VALERIAN. My dear Lessep, do not alarm yourself. I shall not ask you to stay here with me. Indeed, I order you to accompany Mr. Stahl. You would not be the least use to me just now—merely a hindrance. Take him, Stahl, with my warmest recommendation.

STAHL. Valerian, this is suicide. Within twenty-four hours there'll be street fighting here. You know as well as I who they will try to murder first.

VALERIAN. We shall see. If it gets too uncomfortable I suppose I shall have to join Frommer for a while, though I shall dislike that intensely. The man's a bloodthirsty old bore.

LESSEP [beginning to cry]. I can't leave you here, Mr. Valerian.

VALERIAN. Oh, yes, you can. Quite easily. . . . Please spare me these heroics, they do not become you.

STAHL. [looking at his watch]. Heavens, it's late. We

must go at once. If we can't cross the frontier before dawn, we may be fired at. Valerian, for the last time; will you come?

VALERIAN. No.

STAHL. Very well, then. . . . Good-bye.

VALERIAN. Good-bye, my dear Stahl. I shall look forward to your letters about the evils of South America. Please remember me to your wife.

LESSEP [sobbing]. Good-bye, Mr. Valerian.

VALERIAN. Before we part, Lessep, I've one more job for you. Buy Mr. Stahl a new hat.

STAHL [with a burst of nervous impatience, to LESSEP]. For God's sake, man, come—if you're coming! Don't waste your pity on him. He's mad!

[Exit STAHL and LESSEP.]

VALERIAN. There goes marriage! Poor Stahl! Always the subordinate, staggering under the luggage of a social-climbing wife and a playboy son. . . . He'll dislike South America even more than I should. . . . I wonder if he secretly hopes to be taken back, if things go right, here. If he does, he's mistaken. The family is a charming institution, but one has to pay for it. I don't like deserters.

[Takes up house telephone.]

Hullo. . . . Hullo. . . .

[Goes to door, opens it and calls.]

Schwartz!

[No answer. Crosses to door, opens it and calls.]

Schwartz! Frederick! Louis! Kurt!

[*No answer. Comes back to centre of stage.*]
Bolted. . . . Well, I can't blame them. . . . Gone to a demonstration, I suppose, to shout stickjaw slogans with the rest, and listen to their gibbering prophets who promise the millennium in a week.
[*Goes to window.*]
You poor fish, so cock-a-whoop in your little hour of comradeship and hope! I'm really sorry for you. You don't know what you're letting yourselves in for, trying to beat us on our own ground! You will take to machine-guns without having enough. You will imagine that, in a People's Army, it is against your principles to obey orders—and then wonder why it is that, in spite of your superior numbers, you are always beaten. You will count on foreign support and be disappointed, because the international working-class does not read your mosquito journals. It prefers our larger and livelier organs of enlightenment, which can afford snappier sports news, smarter features, and bigger photographs of bathing lovelies. We shall expose your lies and exaggerate your atrocities, and you will be unable to expose or exaggerate ours. The churches will be against you. The world of money and political influence will say of us: "After all, they are the decent people, *our* sort. The others are a rabble." A few of the better educated may go so far as to exclaim: "A plague on both your houses!" Your only open supporters abroad will be a handful of intellectuals, who, for the last twenty years, have signed letters of protest against everything from bi-

metallism in Ecuador to the treatment of yaks in
Thibet. . . .

> [*As he speaks these last lines, he returns to the
> desk and helps himself to a sandwich from a
> plate which is lying there. Enter Storm-
> Trooper* GRIMM, *very quietly.* VALERIAN
> *turns and starts slightly, on seeing him.*]

VALERIAN. To what do I owe this unexpected pleasure?

GRIMM. I startled you, didn't I?

VALERIAN. Yes, for a moment, I confess you did.

GRIMM. That's what I wanted.

VALERIAN. You came up the back staircase? How did
you get in?

GRIMM. The doors are standing open.

VALERIAN. My servants have all run away, it seems.

GRIMM. I knew that. I met one of them in the city.

VALERIAN. So you came to keep me company? Most
considerate. . . . You've brought a message, I suppose?

GRIMM. Yes. I've brought a message.

VALERIAN. Excellent. Does the Leader want me to join
him?

GRIMM. My message isn't from the Leader. But you
may join him. Sooner than you think.

VALERIAN. This all sounds very mysterious. . . . Where
is he now? Still in the capital? Or has he gone to
Frommer? [GRIMM *does not answer.*] Come,
come! We haven't the whole night to waste!

GRIMM. What I have to say to you won't take long.

VALERIAN. So much the better. . . . But first let me offer
you one of these excellent sandwiches. . . .

[*Moves his hand towards the plate.* GRIMM
whips out a pistol and covers him.]

GRIMM. Keep away from that telephone!

VALERIAN [*after recovering from the shock*]. My dear
child, you mustn't wave that thing about! It might
go off.

GRIMM. Get back over there. Against the wall.

VALERIAN [*obeying*]. You little fool! It was the Leader
who told you to do this, I suppose?

GRIMM. The Leader will never tell me to do anything,
again. If you want him, go and look in his study.
You'll find him with his face on the table, and
twenty bullets in his back, and the blood all over
that fine Turkey rug you gave him. . . .

VALERIAN. So? My dear boy, do stop trembling and
slobbering at the mouth in that disgusting manner! To tell you the truth, your news doesn't surprise me quite as much as you'd suppose. I always
suspected that you and your gang of hooligans
would rat, when you thought the time had come.
Only the time *hasn't* come, you see. That's where
you show a deplorable lack of political foresight. . . .

GRIMM. I didn't come here to talk about the Leader.

VALERIAN. I can very well imagine why you came here,
my murderous little gunman. Having lost one master, you're in search of another. . . . Well, as it happens, I can use you quite conveniently. . . . You
have a car with you, I suppose?

GRIMM. What if I have?

VALERIAN. And plenty of petrol? Petrol, in these days,
is worth rubies. My chauffeur seems to have dis-

appeared. I want you to drive me to General Frommer's headquarters, at once.

GRIMM. And if I refuse?

VALERIAN. Oh, I hardly expect you to refuse. . . . After
your little shooting-party, I've no doubt that you
and your colleagues stuffed your pockets with all
the bank-notes in the Leader's safe? You're feeling
quite rich? Well, let me tell you that, across the
frontier, where you will be obliged to travel, very
fast and soon, those notes are practically worth-
less. . . . Now I am prepared to give you ten thousand gold francs. . . .

GRIMM. I don't want your money!

VALERIAN. Fifteen thousand! [GRIMM is silent.] Twenty thousand! [GRIMM is silent.] Oh, you needn't
be suspicious! They're really here, in this room, in
a safe behind the panelling. . . . I'm ready to trust
you, you see. Aren't you being rather unwise to
refuse? Think of the alternative. If Frommer's
men catch you—as, without my protection, they
probably will—you will be hanged, or possibly
burnt alive.

GRIMM. Valerian, the first time we met you thought
you recognized me.

VALERIAN. And you assured me that it was impossible.

GRIMM. I was lying.

VALERIAN. So? Your candour does you credit.

GRIMM. Don't you want to know my name?

VALERIAN. Yes. I think you really do owe me an intro-
duction.

GRIMM. It's Grimm.

VALERIAN. Grimm? Grimm? There are so many Grimms in this country. . . . I seem to remember something. . . .

GRIMM. Five years ago, a boy got a job in your office. A week later, some stamps disappeared. He was the latest employee, so they dismissed him, on suspicion. He appealed to you. You said that you could not reverse your head clerk's decision, and that, in any case, guilty or not, an example must be made. . . .

VALERIAN. Ah, I remember now! An unfortunate case. . . . Well, it may please you to know that the head clerk himself was dismissed a few weeks afterwards. He had been cheating us for years.

GRIMM. Yes, I knew that, too.

VALERIAN. I am delighted to be in a position to make you some tardy amends. . . . Shall we say twenty-five thousand?

GRIMM. You said: "An example must be made."

VALERIAN. Yes. And I should say the same today.

GRIMM. You haven't changed, Valerian. I'm glad of that. I was afraid. . .

VALERIAN. Fascinating as these reminiscences are, don't you think we had better be starting? We can continue this discussion much more conveniently in your car.

GRIMM. I took a lot of trouble to get that post in your office. I had to have it. I had to see what you were like—the man who sent my parents to their graves.

VALERIAN. My dear boy, this is sheer persecution

mania! You should see a doctor. I assure you that I never set eyes on either of your parents in my life!

GRIMM. No, you never set eyes on them. Probably you never set eyes on any of the people who kept those little shops along Grand Avenue. But your big store undersold them, and ruined them all. My father went bankrupt. He shot himself. My mother died soon after.

VALERIAN. I am truly sorry to hear it.

GRIMM. When I was sacked from your office, without references, I couldn't get a job. One day, I was sitting in the park, your park; I hadn't eaten anything for twenty-four hours. There was a meeting going on; a speaker from the Leader's Party. I listened. A night or two later, I heard the Leader himself. He told us how he would smash the big businesses, the chain-stores, the Valerian Trust. He told us how he would help the small men, people like my father. I believed him. I joined the Party.... And then came the National Revolution. We were in power. And it was all lies. The Leader betrayed us. When I realized that, I knew what I had to do. Never mind. That score was settled, at last—tonight....

VALERIAN. Most interesting.... And now, may I ask, why do you come here to tell me all this?

GRIMM. I have come to give you a message. A message from my father and mother, and all those others...

VALERIAN. And the message is—?

GRIMM. You must die.

VALERIAN. I must die. . . . How curious. . . .

GRIMM. Say your prayers, Valerian. If you know any.

VALERIAN. How very curious this is! It's quite true. You are actually able to kill *me!* And you will! Oh, I don't doubt you're in earnest. I know that pale, hatchet-faced look of yours. . . . When I said that I recognized you, I meant, perhaps, that I recognized that look. I recognized Death. We all know him by sight.

GRIMM. Kneel down, damn you! Pray! Pray for forgiveness! Squeal for your life! Kneel, you swine!

VALERIAN. No, my little man. There you are asking too much. I'm afraid I can't give you the pleasure of humiliating me. It simply isn't in you. Be content with what you have. You can kill the great Valerian. What a treat! Don't tremble so, or you'll miss me altogether and hit that statuette, which would be a real disaster. Come on. Don't be afraid. I am waiting. Shoot.

GRIMM [*panting, near to collapse*]. I—I can't!

VALERIAN. You can't? Ah, now, I'm afraid, you're beginning to bore me. I over-estimated you, you see. I have no interest in weaklings.

GRIMM. Get out of my sight, do you hear? Get out!

VALERIAN. Not so fast. You and I have still a good deal to talk about. . . . Put that pistol away and get yourself a drink. You look as if you were going to faint.

GRIMM. Get out, I tell you!

VALERIAN. You think, perhaps, that you might screw up the courage to shoot me in the back? I shall give you no such opportunity. I am quite well aware of the power of the human eye. . . . Now, do pull yourself together. Put it away and let us talk. [GRIMM *does not move.*] Very well. Have it your own way. I can be as patient as you. Probably more so. I think you'll soon get tired of this nonsense. [*A pause.*] Let us pass the time agreeably. Shall I tell you about my crimes? The number of widows I have starved to death? The babies I have trampled under foot? Do I appear to you as a monster with horns? I suppose I do. How strange. . . . Here we are, united, for the moment, by a relationship more intimate than the most passionate embrace, and we see each other as mere caricatures. . . . Are you a human being, too, under your dangerous little reptile skin? No doubt. Have you a sweetheart? I don't think so. In any case, you would soon lose her. Your dreary death-cult is hardly likely to amuse a young lady. . . . Tell me about your mother, though. That's always interesting. I expect you were an only child. Her pet. Born rather late in the marriage. The son who was to achieve wonders. What did she teach you, at nights, beside the cot? What did she whisper?

GRIMM [*screams and shoots*]. Leave my mother alone, you bastard!

> [*He fires three more shots into* VALERIAN'S *prostrate body, kicks it savagely, looks wildly round the room, and rushes out.*]

CURTAIN

(BEFORE THE CURTAIN)

[The five male members of the chorus represent the typical readers of five English newspapers. They should be dressed according to their shades of political opinion. Thus, the FIRST READER has a conservative, highly respectable government paper, the SECOND a violently reactionary, more popular paper, with pictures, the THIRD a liberal paper, the FOURTH a communist paper. The FIFTH READER, who is trembling all over, is studying one of those sensational and alarming news-letters which give the "low-down" on the international situation. Each reader is seated. A spotlight rests on each in turn, as he reads his passage aloud.]

FOURTH READER. Workers rising everywhere. Fascist Collapse.

SECOND READER. General Frommer confident of victory over Reds.

FIRST READER. Tarnberg believed captured by insurgents. Government forces retire on Konia.

SECOND READER. Red Terror in Tarnberg.

THIRD READER. People's Army successful. White troops in retreat.

FOURTH READER. Workers deal smashing blow to international Fascism. Tarnberg cheers march of heroes.

FIFTH READER. From a source usually reliable, we hear that Markov, the Ostnian General, has secretly left Paris to join Westland's General Frommer as military adviser. Subscribers will recall that Markov has long been a valued friend of Frommer's beautiful blonde wife. As told in number 256 of our bulletin, their friendship had a romantic beginning during the Salzburg festival, two years ago, when the gallant Ostnian rescued Her Ladyship's poodle, Jimmy, from a baroque fountain.

THIRD READER. It is important for us to realize that the People's Army is supported not only by the extreme Left, but by all the Liberal and progressive elements in Westland. If they win, Westland will once more take her place among the democratic countries.

SECOND READER. Inhuman cruelties by Reds. Bishop boiled alive. British governess' terrible experience.

FOURTH READER. Mass executions in Kresthaufen. Fascist thugs machine-gun women and children.

FIFTH READER. An interesting sidelight on relations between Frommer and the City is thrown from Mayfair. Lady Corker, well-known local right-wing socialite, gave an al-fresco supper-party on Thursday last, at which the Westland Ambassador was guest of honour. In the charades which followed, His Excellency and the Chairman of the Anglo-

Saurian Oil Co. made a sensation as Darnley and the Queen of Scots.

SECOND READER. Church denounces Communism. World-wide day of prayer ordered for better industrial relations.

THIRD READER. Christianity and Socialism should be allies, says East-End Vicar.

FIRST READER. Tension in Europe increases. Prime Minister to announce British plan for mediation.

SECOND READER. No Bolshevism in Europe, say Anti-Comintern Powers. War material pouring in to Reds from Russia.

FOURTH READER. International Fascism alarmed. Foreign tanks to crush Westland workers.

THIRD READER. Intervention threatened by totalitarian states. League summoned.

FIRST READER. There is an increasing danger of Europe splitting into two irreconcilable camps. To this, the Englishman, with his love of liberty and his distrust of cast-iron ideologies, is tempted to retort, in the words of our national poet: "A plague on both your houses!"

FIFTH READER. From War Offices sources comes the news that the outbreak of world war cannot possibly be delayed beyond the middle of March. . . . [*Covers his face with his hands.*] Oh dear! Oh dear! Oh dear!

BLACK OUT

ACT THREE

SCENE III

[*The stage is quite bare, with the light-circle, as in the dream-scene in Act Two, Scene I. But with this difference: in the extreme corners of the stage are two dimly illuminated beds, containing motionless, unrecognizable figures, over which, in each corner, a doctor and a nurse are bending. These parts are doubled by the actors playing* DR. THORVALD *and* HILDA THORVALD, *and* COLONEL HUSSEK *and* MRS. VRODNY. *There is a screen at the head of each bed.*]

LEFT DOCTOR. Yes, Sister? What is it?

LEFT NURSE. This chest-wound case, Doctor. He's had another haemorrhage.

LEFT DOCTOR. Let me see. . . . Hm. . . . There's nothing I can do, I'm afraid. He's sinking. What's his name?

LEFT NURSE. Eric Thorvald, Doctor.

LEFT DOCTOR. Poor fellow. Knew his father slightly. Clever man. Bit conceited.

RIGHT DOCTOR. What's her name?

RIGHT NURSE. Anna Vrodny. One of our best nurses. Do you think she'll pull through, Doctor?

RIGHT DOCTOR. Not a chance. She won't last the night.
Move her out as soon as it's over, Sister. We're
terribly short of beds.

> [ERIC and ANNA, *dressed and made up exact-*
> *ly as in Act Two, Scene I, emerge from be-*
> *hind the screens at the heads of their respec-*
> *tive beds, and advance into the light-circle.*
> *The beds fade into darkness.*]

ERIC. Anna, is that you?

ANNA. Yes, Eric.

ERIC. Come closer. I can't see you clearly.

ANNA. Where are you? Your voice sounds so faint.

ERIC. Standing at the barricade
The swift impartial bullet
Selected and struck.
This is our last meeting.

ANNA. Working in the hospital
Death shuffled round the beds
And brushed me with his sleeve.
I shall not see you again.

> [*A distant noise of shots and shouting.*]

ANNA. Will people never stop killing each other?
There is no place in the world
For those who love.

ERIC. Believing it was wrong to kill,
I went to prison, seeing myself
As the sane and innocent student
Aloof among practical and violent madmen,
But I was wrong. We cannot choose our world,
Our time, our class. None are innocent, none.

Causes of violence lie so deep in all our lives
It touches every act.
Certain it is for all we do
We shall pay dearly. Blood
Will mine for vengeance in our children's hap-
      piness,
Distort our truth like an arthritis.
Yet we must kill and suffer and know why.
All errors are not equal. The hatred of our
      enemies
Is the destructive self-love of the dying,
Our hatred is the price of the world's freedom.
This much I learned from prison. This struggle
Was my struggle. Even if I would
I could not stand apart. And after
Sighting my rifle for the necessary wrong,
Afraid of death, I saw you in the world,
The world of faults and suffering and death,
The world where love has its existence in our
      time,
Its struggle with the world, love's source and
      object.

ANNA. I saw it too.
      Working in the wards
      Among the material needs of the dying
      I found your love
      And did not need to call you.

ERIC. We could not meet.

ANNA. They were too strong.
      We found our peace

        Only in dreams.

ERIC. As irresponsible and generalized phantoms
        In us love took another course
        Than the personal life.

ANNA. In sorrow and death
        We tasted love.

ERIC. But in the lucky guarded future
        Others like us shall meet, the frontier gone,
        And find the real world happy.

ANNA. The place of love, the good place.
        O hold me in your arms.
        The darkness closes in.
        [*The lights fade slowly. Background of music.*]

ERIC. Now as we come to our end,
        As the tiny separate lives
        Fall, fall to their graves,
        We begin to understand.

ANNA. A moment, and time will forget
        Our failure and our name
        But not the common thought
        That linked us in a dream.

ERIC. Open the closing eyes,
        Summon the failing breath,
        With our last look we bless
        The turning maternal earth.

ANNA. Europe lies in the dark
        City and flood and tree;
        Thousands have worked and work
        To master necessity.

ERIC. To build the city where

        The will of love is done
        And brought to its full flower
        The dignity of man.
ANNA.   Pardon them their mistakes,
        The impatient and wavering will.
        They suffer for our sakes,
        Honour, honour them all.
BOTH.   Dry their imperfect dust,
        The wind blows it back and forth.
        They die to make man just
        And worthy of the earth.

                    CURTAIN